The story of a PBP year

Malcolm Dancy

Contents

A Somewhat Self-Indulgent Preamble

In 2012 my New Year's resolution was to cycle at least 500km in each calendar month, part of an endeavour to be fitter. It was a very small commitment given that, with an 8km each way commute to work, I was doing 350km to start with. What with a bit of riding to and fro for transport at the weekend, all I was really committing myself to was a couple of moderate rides, or one long ride, once a month.

My resolution was something of a success. I enjoyed counting the kilometres (and kilometres are more enjoyable to count than miles — you get more for your money). I enjoyed ticking off January February March etc., the sense of achievement with 567, 532, 612 kilometres, and a real back-slapping sense of well-being if I counted over 600. I would cycle to and from work making happy calculations in my head, constantly studying the odometer. Sometimes I went the long way home.

I didn't complete the calendar year. That said, I'm not going to judge the success of the year-long challenge by the simple yes or no of whether I achieved it. September came in just below 500km and November and October fell further short. That I *averaged* more than 500km per month was a consolation, but the success was that the challenge of kilometre-counting added an extra dimension to my cycling and got me doing more of it.

It wasn't a big deal. But it was more significant than the year before, when I gave up eating penguins (the chocolate bar — not eating the large flightless bird is unrealistically easy for anyone not stranded in the Antarctic.) The reason was that I love chocolate but need to eat less of it. I'm lucky enough (and also unlucky) to work in a place where biscuits are freely available during the morning break. Penguins are not my favourite chocolate bar, but I would eat them if they were all that was available. In this way my resolution did cut down on my chocolate consumption, albeit not by much.

I have kept going with this resolution, and it's now in its fifth year. So far my annual distances are 6000, 7500, 8800, and 8500km, the increases above 6000km mostly due to multistage long distance audax[1] events, but I have yet to get through twelve consecutive months without a low mileage blip. Some years due to pieces being cut out of my arm, or crashes, and some years due to lethargy. One year, and perhaps this one, I will succeed.

---

[1] There's a glossary. But if you don't know this word, maybe I could help you by selling you my earlier book, *A Virgin Discovers Long Distance Cycling*, available as a paperback on Amazon for just £4.99, or on Kindle for just £1.99.

INTRODUCTION

This is the story of a PBP year. PBP is the acronym for Paris Brest Paris, a long-distance cycling event that takes place every four years and draws 6000 odd cyclists (some of them very odd) to ride the 1200km there and back — Brest is the westernmost tip of France – in four days, averaging 13⅔ km/h. The 18th event of this kind took place between August 17th and 21st 2015. It was my first such ride, and this is why I am motivated to write about it, but most people who ride have ridden it before. Another way of putting it is that most who ride it will do so again.

All those 6000 riders had to qualify during the previous eight months by riding regulated audax events of 200km, 300km, 400km and 600km[2] to prove themselves worthy of entry. Those events themselves were closely scrutinised to ensure riders did indeed cover the appropriate distances without resource to shortcuts or motor assistance. Illegal drug taking is not monitored. We are talking amateurs here.

PBP was started up in 1901 to sell newspapers. This was quite the thing in France at the time. It was so successful the organisers were inspired to run another similar but longer event, a race around the hexagon of France which they called, unremarkably, the *Tour de France*, and which became even more famous. But PBP (the full name doesn't trip off the tongue quite as easily as *le Tour*) continues to hold an iconic status among a certain breed of cyclist. In 1910 Peugeot, then a well-known bicycle manufacturer, entered a car in the event by special arrangement. The idea was to show that the cars they had recently started to manufacture were so reliable that not only could they complete such an enormous distance, but that they could do so without major breakdown and even compete with a bicycle. The car did so, managing a creditable 10th fastest time.

Over the years, PBP continued, although not without some operational difficulties. These include the two world wars that engulfed France among so many other countries, but also the loss of professional riders, who preferred to ride the more lucrative *Tour*, and a split in the

---

[2] Kilometres are preferred to miles for audax, since the audax movement started in France. Plus the more for your money thing.

organisation that has given us two separate organisations running separate PBP events, some-times in the same year. In this volume we will only be concerned with the *Audax Club Parisien* version.

I had heard of PBP soon after I discovered cycle sport. As a young man, I competed in a few amateur races, a lot of time trails, and read about heroes of epic classics such as Paris-Roubaix and Liège-Bastogne-Liège, and of course of *le Tour*. I knew that PBP was no longer a profes-sional race, but clearly it was still meant for superhumans.

It would be my third long-distance audax event. (For these purposes long-distance means 1000km or more — something that will be undertaken over a period of 4 to 5 days.) My first, London Edinburgh London 2013, was a challenge and a goal and finally a revelation to me. I loved the event. I loved it so much I wrote a book about it. As I may have mentioned.

While riding LEL I met lots of people who had ridden PBP. In fact quite a percentage of LEL riders have done PBP, and all of them said it was wonderful, an amazing experience, unlike anything else, incomparable. Stuff like that. I knew right away I was going to do it.

The following summer, 2014, I had the intention to ride from Land's End to John O'Groats (LEJOG if you like your acronyms). Going cycling for a five-day period in July had set a precedent. My Good Lady had granted her blessing and enjoyed following my progress online, so doing something similar the following year made sense in terms of family dynamics. I was planning to do LEJOG, until I noticed a 1300km audax ride in the Highlands of Scotland[3] and planned for that instead. So, on five days during a heatwave, I cycled from Arran, up the West Coast, across the north coast as far as Tongue, and down through the Great Glen and Glencoe, sleeping in a small municipal park in Oban, in a ditch somewhere in Sutherland, on the beach at Durness with a view towards the Arctic, and in a bus shelter near Loch Ness, catching seven ferries and climbing 10,000m — which is more than you'd climb on an ascent of Everest, although no one has done that by bike. I'll come back to Everest later.

These two long-distance audax rides, LEL and HGWI, couldn't have been more differ-ent; LEL had over 1000 riders, almost as many volunteers, and brilliantly run controls between each stage, providing all the food you'd need to eat and a place to sleep; the HGWI was X-rated. X-rated has nothing to do with sex in this case, but instead means that only a minimum of facilities is provided. It is regarded as the purest form of audax by the people most in favour of it. The HGWI ride offered its 35 riders no support at all except for one bunkhouse with food

---

[3] The Highlands, Glens and Western Isles 1300km Audax organised by Mark Rigby.

and shelter in the desolate middle of Highland Scotland. Otherwise riders had to fend for themselves, and at the end of each stage had to procure evidence in the form of a receipt that they had indeed arrived within the allotted time. Sleeping and eating arrangements were entirely up to the riders.

In terms of self-sufficiency, or the lack of it, PBP would be close to LEL. In terms of numbers, it is much bigger, although this is something that might change over the next 50 years.

To ride PBP it is necessary to qualify, as I said. This qualification involves four long rides and a total of at least 1500km, all within audax time limits. The purpose of this is to ensure that people do not turn up for such a big ride without preparation. For LEL there is no such requirement. Interestingly, the completion rate for the two rides are similar. But the necessity to qualify demands a degree of planning.

I like planning cycle rides. For one thing, it is a lot easier than actually cycling. I like looking at maps and picturing myself covering roads that sound cool and exotic, building up mileages. This is what I planned:

200km: The Ghan – London-Oxford-London

300km: Oasts and Coasts — a tour of Kent

400km: "Porkers" a tour of steeper parts of Dorset.

600km: Bryan Chapman – South Wales to North Wales and back again

I also intended to ride the Ditchling Devil in June (200km), the Dunwich Dynamo, in July (not an audax, but 200km nonetheless), to compete in the Mersey Wheelers 24-hour time trial, and to take a bicycle with me on a planned ten-day family holiday in Majorca. That and riding to work.

With the exception of the Ditchling Devil ride in June, none of these rides began within 10km of where I live in South West London, and only half of them started within 100km. Considering that 20% of the population of the United Kingdom, and 25% of the population of England, live in the London area, this is surprising as well as inconvenient. It might be that the sheer number of people living in London, and the fact that Londoners have more space per capita than the citizens of most European metropolitan areas, coupled with the apparent need for every adult to own a car, means that anywhere close to London is crap for recreational long distance cycling.

Part of the planning involved logistics. Events starting at 8 o'clock in the morning on a location distant from my home on Saturday require a very early start, and often driving there.

7

In this way I am contributing to the Autogeddon[4] that blights the lives of so many of us. A better man and a better cyclist than me would harden up and cycle to the start, thinking the extra hundred kilometre round trip was all good preparation. But.

Before LEL in 2013 I needed to consider how I would approach the event, how I would get myself into a sufficient degree of fitness to make it possible, and what kind of bicycle I would need for the journey. Two years later, it was much easier. Firstly I knew I could do it; I thought I had made sufficient mistakes in previous long distance events I now knew what to do. To some extent there was no need to plan much in the way of training rides, since the qualifiers I would have to do would make up the bulk of the training. And I already had the bike, a beautiful bike.

I think it is the duty of any cyclist to have a beautiful bike if they can. It's a question of setting an example, promoting a positive image for a healthy lifestyle.

There is a counter argument. The majority of my adventure cycling heroes exhort people to just get out on their bikes and do it anyway, and I do see this. There is certainly no need to wait until you can afford a decent bike before you start cycling. Lance Armstrong,[5] who is no longer anyone's hero, said famously in the title of his autobiography that "it's not about the bike,"[6] but sometimes it is. And Armstrong always rode with state-of-the-art bikes as well as state-of-the-art drugs.

The bike I have been riding for the last two years was hand-built in Hackney by Ryan McCabe, who runs Oak Cycles. I have bought cars for less than the cost of this bike, but these cars were long ago reduced to scrap metal, and I intend to be riding my Oak until I reach an age and a state of decrepitude where I can no longer balance on two wheels, when perhaps I shall give it to a grandchild yet unborn. It is not a very fast bike, which is my fault not Ryan's, because I chose to weigh it down with the items I consider essential, but it is comfortable. My bike is perfect for everyweather long-distance cycling and general everyday transport, and yet it is difficult if not impossible to buy bikes off the peg with this kind of specification. To wit,

---

[4] Actually this is the title of an excellent book-length poem by Heathcote Williams.

[5] In November 2012 I was cycling one afternoon through the village of Edenbridge in Kent. The village's famous bonfire had already been built in preparation for Guy Fawkes night, and the guy, the effigy to be burnt, was a giant representation of Lance Armstrong wearing a Jim'll Fix It badge.

[6] I hope future editions of the book, perhaps revised from a prison cell, will be subtitled "It's All About the Drugs and the Lying."

a drop handlebar road bike with clearance for wide tyres and mudguards,[7] disc brakes,[8] hub gears, and dynamo lighting. On this bike I'm happy to ride all day or all night and perhaps both, and I'm happy to ride it on any kind of road and on most bridleways.

---

[7] Call me soft. I can't bear to cycle with a wet arse, let alone a strip of muddy water up my back. I'm not keen on road spray in the face either.

[8] I had an accident recently on my hack bike while commuting home from work. On a sunny afternoon with perfect visibility, a driver failed to see me and pulled out into my path. The hack bike had cheap centre-pull brakes, and could not stop me fast enough to avoid a collision. The accident was the driver's fault, as my solicitor was able to show, but the pain was mine.

CHAPTER ONE

Other People

While I was planning my riding, others were out already doing it.

Steve "Teethgrinder" Abraham was engaged in an audacious attempt to beat a record for the greatest distance cycled in a calendar year. It was quite a record to beat; Tommy Goodwin managed 75,065 miles in 1939.

Godwin rode a state-of-the-(then)-art bike provided by the Raleigh Bicycle Company, with Sturmey-Archer gears that weighed in at more than 14 kg, a bike built for reliability rather than speed. He was riding on roads that were poorly surfaced compared to today's conditions, but also largely empty of traffic. By the end of October he had already broken the record, previously standing at 62,658 miles, and he did so in style, riding into Trafalgar Square to a rapturous reception. He rode through the winter, and as war came, he taped up his lights to provide the minimum necessary illumination during the blackouts. After having set his "unbeatable" record, he continued until May 1940, when after 500 days' riding he secured the 100,000-mile (160,000 km) record as well. After this he needed to spend a couple of weeks learning how to walk again before he was able to join the RAF and the war effort.

To give you an idea of what kind of distance 76 065 miles is, it is the equivalent of 86 separate journeys from Land's End to John O'Groats. Each journey would take four days and there would be no rest between them. For the benefit of those readers more familiar with North American geography than British, it is 31 times the distance from Los Angeles to New York, each trans-American trip taking just over 12 days.

Steve was aiming to ride an average of 205 miles every day. He was taking a year off work to meet this challenge, and was backed by a team of volunteers, who organised everything from sponsorship to donations, providing food accommodation and maintenance, not to mention washing his kit.

He got himself off to a cracking start. Beginning at midnight on New Year's Eve, while I was outside a Thames-side pub watching fireworks, he pedalled off into the night. At 10 o'clock that morning, while I was very much asleep, he took part in a club 10 mile time trial. By the end of the day he had clocked 222 miles. Three weeks later, he had accomplished 4276 miles, or the best part of five Land's End to John O'Groats. On the same date in 1939, Tommy Goodwin had done just 3645.

Tommy Goodwin being congratulated for a record that would stand for 76 years.

All was going well for Steve until he was in collision with a moped in March, resulting in a fractured ankle. The sensible thing to have done at this point would have been to call it a day, perhaps aiming to make another attempt the following year. Accept the slings and mopeds of outrageous fortune. Et cetera. The heroic thing, however... After a moderate period of healing, Steve found he was able to pedal with just one leg. He was unable to balance, but that was okay because he managed to get ICE tricycles to lend him a three-wheel tadpole-design[9] recumbent trike, adapted for use with one leg only, with support for his other leg in plaster, and was able to find a place to ride off-road, namely Milton Keynes Bowl, where he did thousands of circuits. As he was on Strava, anybody with an internet connection could see his daily grinding one-legged rides, 90 miles a day, going in circles (or ovals to be pedantic). When his leg was mended enough he could ride a bicycle again, he could be seen at audax events with his crutch strapped to the frame of his bicycle for those times when he needed to walk. Later he would estimate that the injury set him back 10,000 miles.

He was not alone in chasing this dream. Over in the States Kurt Searvogel had the same idea. Kurt had one big advantage in that he lived in Florida, where it is significantly more conducive to cycling, at least in winter. During these winter months, as Steve was clocking up more miles than Tommy Goodwin had done on the same days 76 years earlier, Kurt was clocking up still more. Steve was banking on his daily mileages growing as the weather got better, which is precisely what happened in 1939 to Tommy Goodwin. It is simply easier to ride long distances when it is warm enough to wear shorts instead of multiple layers and overshoes.

In January 2015 Tom Davies set off from his home in Earlsfield, South-West London, intending to be the youngest person to cycle around the world. I knew Tom because I had taught him A level physics over the two previous years. He set off in January in one of the coldest winters for a long time, especially in southern Europe.

There are rules for cycling around the world. Strictly speaking they are for the purposes of the Guinness Book of Records, and only matter if you are trying to set the record for the fastest circumnavigation, but many of the hundreds of people who cycle the globe since Thomas Stevens did it first in 1886 on a penny farthing[10] have chosen to follow them. The rules are as follows:

You cycle in a continuous direction either East to West or West to East[11].

You cover at least 18,000 miles,

You pass through two antipodal points.

The antipodal points are my favourite bit. Two points that are exactly opposite to one another on the globe, so a straight line between them would pass through the centre of the earth.

---

[9] This means the two wheels are at the front.

[10] Setting a precedent, he wrote a book about the adventure: "Around the World on a Bicycle." He didn't have a blog though.

[11] And everybody goes east, because that's the direction the prevailing westerly winds go

Obviously the north and south poles make for one pair, although not a useful one considering the logistical difficulties of travelling to either. Useful examples include Madrid, Spain and Wellington, New Zealand, and Beijing, China and Bahia Blanca, Argentina.

Much to Tom's annoyance, the Guinness organisation, arbiters of all things world record related, as well as purveyors of the famous stout, refuse to acknowledge records for the youngest person to do this sort of thing, feeling it is reckless to encourage dangerous activities, especially if they involve, or are likely to involve, minors. Tom was 19, but subsequent record attempts would presumably be made by pre-teens. The case of Laura Dekker, a Dutch sailor who defied not only the Guinness Book of Records but the Dutch government and social care system to sail around the globe single-handed at the age of 14 is a case in point. Dutch social services had in fact tried to take her into care, arguing that her parents, by permitting her to do this, were guilty of neglect.

Tom was fairly racing through his journey, generally completing more than 100 miles each day, and was in India by March.

I had bumped into Richard Evans in April the year before, while riding to work. We'd been at the same advance stop line at traffic lights, both of us on fixed wheel bikes with audax UK stickers on the mudguards. Conversation ensued, during which I learned he was about to embark on his midlife crisis ride around the world. The following week. He passed me his card with details of a website. He did indeed set off the next Tuesday, riding what he describes as a deckchair with wheels, his recumbent bicycle. I am quite an accomplished armchair round-the-world cyclist, and Richard's deckchair journey was added to my list of blogs to follow, along with Emily Chappell, Alastair Humphreys, Sarah Orton and Tom Allen, so I could read about his somewhat intimidating catalogue of high mileage days and enthusiastic beer consumption.

These people inspired me to at least want to achieve greatness (or at least impressive distances) on a bicycle. An interview Steve Abraham did – I think it was in the Telegraph – told me about the Eddington number, something that piqued my interest as a physics teacher.

Sir Arthur Eddington was a British physicist whose most important work was in the field of astrophysics and in the popularisation of science. He was perhaps most famous for leading an expedition to be the first observer of a total eclipse after the end of the First World War, with the purpose of testing the bending of light around the sun according to the general theory of relativity published by Albert Einstein in 1916. His popular writings on science made him a household name in the United Kingdom. For example he was the author of the idea that an

13

infinite number of monkeys strumming on typewriters might write all the books in the British Museum[12]. He is also responsible for a measure of a long-distance cyclist's riding achievements. You work out your Eddington number by finding the maximum number for which you have cycled that number of miles that number of times. For example, if you have cycled a ride of exactly 50 miles 50 times that would give you an Eddington number of 50. But to increase it to 51, none of your 50 mile rides would count. Eddington himself achieved an Eddington number of 84 before he died of cancer at the early age of 61. My own number would be somewhere between 70 and 90, but I don't have very clear records of rides I did in my youth, hence the vagueness. [13]

Curiously, converting an Eddington number from miles to kilometres is not a simple procedure. Our hypothetical rider, who has ridden exactly 50 miles 50 times, would have ridden 80km 50 times as well, but unless he had 30 other rides to consider, his kilometre Eddington number would remain at 50. His hypothetical sister, on the other hand, who has only done 45 mile rides, i.e. 72 km, but done 70 of them, would have a kilometre Eddington number of 70, although her mile Eddington number (45) was lower than her brother's.

Professional riders presumably all have Eddington numbers in the hundreds. While I was planning to ride PBP and marking event dates on the calendar in the kitchen, Tour de France riders like Chris Froome and Alberto Contador were putting in long training rides.

---

[12] The meme has evolved so that it is now the works of Shakespeare (obviously a small subset of the books of the British Museum) that the monkeys write.

[13] According to the journalist writing about Steve Abraham, Steve's number at the time was 127, and this was towards the start of his record attempt, so it will have grown considerably since then.

CHAPTER TWO

The Steam Ride

On 15th March I completed my first big ride of the year, and my first qualifying event for PBP, something described as the *Steam Ride: London-Oxford-London (LOL)*, and also, somewhat confusingly, as *The Ghan*. My friend Wikipedia tells me that The Ghan is an Australian passenger train service between Adelaide and Darwin which takes three days to travel the 3000 kilometres, including a four-hour stopover in Alice Springs. Ghan is short for Afghan Express, originally a nickname given by the crew of the train in honour of Afghan camel drivers who helped explore the country's interior. Nothing so very much to do with cycling, but a clue to a theme in the mind of the ride's organiser, who had put together something to appeal to that seldom commented upon breed of cyclists, the cycling train-spotter. The 200km route, one I hoped would be less epic than a journey across the Australian outback, gave the rider the opportunity to see steam trains at Ruislip Lido Railway, the Cholsey & Wallingford Railway, the Chinnor & Princes Risborough Railway, and Didcot Steam Railway and Museum.

Unfortunately the first of these railways is not connected to the national rail network (i.e. the one run by Network Rail) so I drove to Ruislip. I didn't cycle to Ruislip because I was too much of a wuss to get up an extra hour and a half earlier and to add an extra 70km round trip, but I was hoping that rides like this would make me less of a wuss.

My only association with Ruislip is Leslie Thomas's humorous novel *Tropic of Ruislip* which I read as a spotty adolescent. The Lido there does not feature in the novel, but was originally a reservoir to provide water for the Grand Junction Canal, which it did until 1851. The 60 acre lake was opened in 1933 as a lido for swimming and boating, and in 1945 the narrow gauge railway was built there as an additional attraction. The Dr Who actor Jon Pertwee used to come water-skiing here, and in 1958 a (small) replica of the Titanic was sank in its waters for the film *A Night to Remember*. It's a pretty enough place for an afternoon visit, but nowadays neither boating nor swimming are permitted, which strains the definition of the word lido.

Anyway it was too cold to be swimming.

I arrived in good time for the start except that the car park was a kilometre from the event HQ at Woody Bay Station, and inevitably, I left something important in the car (sunglasses) and had to go back for it (them).

The ride starts along the southern part of the lake (four times in my case) and then skirts around the Colne Valley Regional Park in a generally north-westerly direction, into the rolling chalk landscape of the Chilterns. There were kites in the air, the birds, rather than the contraptions of fabric and string named after them. These birds, once extinct in England, were reintroduced here in the early 1990s.

After 28km we passed through the village of Great Missenden, where Roahl Dahl lived and wrote, and I recognised the great man's local library from a visit I'd made the year before with Junior and My Good Lady. Around 50km we passed Stoke Mandeville, location of the famous and infamous hospital — founded to fight cholera and other infectious diseases, later repurposed as a centre for spinal injuries, and where the Stoke Mandeville Games, precursors to the modern Paralympics were born. Of course it was also beneficiary of Jimmy Saville's charity fundraising and the place where the man sexually abused more than 50 women and girls.

The first control was at Quainton, whose name comes from old English and means Queens Estate (queen Edith, wife of Edward the Confessor) rather than quaint town, although it *is* fairly quaint, and boasts a working windmill at the back of the village green. The control was in the Memorial Hall.

After Quainton, the route took us in an anticlockwise loop, crossing over itself before heading south and west towards Oxford. The ride went right through the centre of Oxford, giving a good view of the dreaming spires, and the traffic and shops exactly like the shops in any other town. The second control was at the Head of the River pub by a bridge over the Thames. By now it was lunchtime on a gloriously sunny spring day and the patio between the road and the pub was packed with people enjoying lunch, most of them cyclists, but a significant minority civilians.

The sight of pint glasses of ale in the sunshine is always tempting, but there was no time for this. I had a lunch appointment. I got the stamp on my brevet card and continued onwards, southwards on very familiar roads to Abingdon.

The name Abingdon is Saxon and means Æbba's hill. Æbba is a Saxon name, and I've no idea how to pronounce it, although I assume it is not the same as the Swedish pop supergroup. The Saxon abbey was founded in the seventh century here, but there is no hill in Abingdon, which lies on the River Thames, so historians believe the Abbey was founded on a nearby hill and later moved. Once the county town of Berkshire, the thriving market town of Abingdon stopped thriving with the growth of the railways, since the main railway didn't come here, going instead through Reading. Reading is now the county town of Berkshire, and Abingdon was shunted into Oxfordshire in 1974. Here we avoided the one-way system through a succession of cycle paths and footpaths that took us past the abbey.

From Abingdon, through Sutton Courtenay, where George Orwell is buried, along with former Prime Minister Herbert Asquith, and where Matilda, daughter of King Henry I, was born in 1102. Matilda married another Henry, son of yet another Henry, who was the Holy Roman Emperor Henry IV. Her Henry became the Holy Roman Emperor Henry V and she became Empress Matilda. Then her Henry died, and Matilda returned to Normandy, which is where kings of England lived at the time. Upon Henry's death (Henry I as opposed to IV or V) Matilda was his heir, but her cousin Stephan claimed the throne and held onto it despite a civil war. Nevertheless, on Stephen's death Matilda's eldest son, obviously called Henry, became Henry II, king of England.

From Sutton Courtenay, the ride followed a cycle path around the back of Didcot Power Station to Didcot. Didcot's enormous power station was built in 1968, not very long after I was. It dominates the landscape, its main chimney 200m tall, and was always the first thing I could see as a child looking out for home when my family were returning from anywhere, a set of huge concrete curves on the horizon, lines of smoke and steam trailing from them in the prevailing wind. The summer before, three of the six cooling towers had been demolished, the main power station having ceased operation in 2013. The demolition took place at 5am despite a large local petition for it to be done in daylight hours, the operators wanting to avoid having to deal with large numbers of spectators. Thousands turned up anyway.

Didcot is a place very close to my heart. I grew up in two of its surrounding villages,[14] Harwell and Appleford, and went to school there. My parents live there now. When I was 17 I spent four weeks of a summer holiday working for a company subcontracted to remove scaffolding used for some purpose unknown inside the power station's enormous boiler house. I used to come home and need two baths to get myself clean at the end of each day. (We didn't

---

[14] One after the other, rather than concurrently.

have a shower.) An insignificant village until 1839, the arrival of Isabard Kingdom Brunel's Great Western Railway changed everything. Brunel wanted to put the London to Bristol line through the town of Abingdon, which would have made it cheaper to build, as well as maintaining Abingdon's prosperity, but a local landowner blocked the railway from passing through there, and Brunel put it through Didcot, building the station in 1844. A later branch line to Oxford increased the town's importance. From a population of a few hundred, it grew to many thousands before I was born, and has continued to grow since, so that it is at least four times the size it was when I went to school there. And it's still growing.

I met Matt at the control outside Didcot Parkway station. It's called Parkway because the station has a large car park to serve those poor souls who drive to the station to catch the morning train to London and maintain their positions in the rat race. I first met Matt on the Isle of Arran at the start of the HGWI event, when he was wearing a Didcot Phoenix Cycling Club cap. He lives in Didcot, but like the vast majority of the town's population, does not come from there.

After chatting to Matt for a few minutes, I left the ride for a detour to my parent's place where I was treated to an excellent lunch, my mother being well aware of the size of a cyclist's appetite. We talked about family stuff, about the weather, of course, and about the very loud bump in the night when the cooling towers came down. The event counted as a minor earthquake. The day after the demolition there had been a thick layer of dust on the car. Presumably there had been dust everywhere else, but the car was a place it needed to be cleaned off of. I had a very pleasant couple of hours with Mum and Dad and then had to make my way back onto the road.

I would spend the rest of the day riding solo, as I expected. Anyone I met on the road now would be moving at a pace much slower than mine. I prefer cycling with company, but cycling on your own is also fun, and it was a small price to pay for lunch with Mum and Dad.

The route took me east now, through Wallingford, the town in whose hospital I was born, and whose name therefore will be forever on my passport. Wallingford is a pretty market town over the Thames, whose historic bridge isn't wide enough for two cars to pass, so there is always a queue at the lights as eastbound and westbound traffic take turns.

After Wallingford I was back in the Chilterns, passing RAF Benson, the oddly named Christmas Common, to Chinnor, where the control was at a petrol station. The road climbed steeply out of Chinnor along the aptly named Hill Road, the summit of which was in the deep shade of the trees lining the road. The road led down from there to High Wycombe, where both Terry Pratchett and Heston Blumenthal went to school. After 183km there was an information control (I will forgive you for using the glossary here). In Burnham Beeches, an ancient beech wood forest used in more than one Harry Potter film, I needed Google Maps to find the secluded cycle path.

From here there were only 20km left to ride, but these were 20km from legs that were suffering. By now the sun had gone and the day had gone with it so I needed my lights. It was cooling off and I needed to put a jacket on, and I was very much looking forward to being home. But the light wind was at my back, and, jacket retrieved, I was warm, and despite not having ridden a bike particularly since the summer, I was finding I could at least do a 200 without undue suffering.

One last information control at Denham Station inside the Coln Valley Regional Park, and a further twenty minutes and I was back at the Ruislip Lido.

CHAPTER THREE

Oasts And Coasts Ride

An oast or oast house is a Kentish architectural phenomenon, a weirdly shaped brick building with the roof the shape of a witch's hat. Oasts were, and perhaps still are, built for the drying of hops prior to their use in the brewing industry, with a kiln on the ground floor creating the hot air to flow upwards past the hops. The hat is a cowl that turns with the wind and draws the hot air up through the building. A coast is the edge of the land where it meets the sea. Kent has an abundance of both oasts and coast and this ride celebrated the fact with a big anti-clockwise loop of the county, making a very satisfactory shape on the map.

This was another event that necessitated a drive to the start; the ride was due to commence at six in the morning, so I had to be on the road at 4:30. I had everything bar the bike in the car ready, and crept out of the house without so much as a cup of tea or glass of juice, putting the bike on the bike rack and setting off. Meopham in Kent, where the event was based, is a short blast around the M25 from where I live, and at this hour there was little traffic to slow a would-be audaxer.

Meopham, pronounced Mepam or Mepum, has the distinction of being the longest village in Europe, with its approximately 6000 residents distributed over 7 miles. The name comes from *Meapaham*, meaning Meapa's village. Whoever Meapa was, his village was first recorded in 788AD.

To make up for such an early kick-off, the organiser had breakfast available from five o'clock, so once I arrived I could get to work on my calorie intake. I was there in good time to relax for a while once I'd accomplished breakfast, but it was probably for the best that there was not so much spare time I could be tempted to lie down and fall asleep.

From the start, we rode just 11km before the earliest of checkpoints at Farningham where we riders had our brevet cards stamped but nobody bothered writing down a time. The point of the checkpoint was simply to force us to go north-east to pick up the scenic route across the

Ashdown Forest rather than going more directly down to Uckfield and saving maybe 5km. In PBP year, it seems that audaxers cannot be trusted.

After a couple of hours' gentle riding and 65km, Poppins Café in Uckfield provided a decent second breakfast, and we could help ourselves to a sticker to confirm our presence.

From there, the ride took us due east to Battle, site of the Battle of Hastings, where once I watched an enthusiastic re-enactment of the event by 100 men in chain mail on its 950th anniversary. Now there was tea and coffee and the option of cake, although no cake quite so dainty as the one on the brevet card stamp.

Now we went along the ancient Weald Way, along Cackle Street, Udimore Lane and through Cock Marling, and I mention these places for no reason other than the pleasure of their names. Cock Marling was originally Coccel Maere Ing, meaning Cockle-rich Sea Fort, the fort part of a ring of such to defend the kingdom of Kent in the fifth century. Since then the sea has retreated steadily, forcing the sea forts to move to the south and east with it. We followed the road to Rye, where we arrived on Cinqueports Street, passed the Cinqueports pub, and were quickly out of town on Fishmarket Road and onto the A259 towards New Romney, sadly missing the town walls and the view of the lowlands to the south. This was the coast in the twelfth century, when the lowlands were the sea, and Rye was a port.

Cinque is five in Old French, and the five ports in Kent and Sussex established by Royal Charter in 1155 were required to maintain ships ready for the Crown in the event of military necessity, in return for certain privileges. These privileges included exemption from taxes and a degree of self-sufficiency with regard to crime and punishment, which allowed for a lucrative trade in smuggling. The original towns were Hastings, New Romney, Hythe, Dover, and Sandwich, but Rye substituted for New Romney when New Romney was damaged by storms and silted up.

The route kept us inland, crossing Romney Marsh as we headed towards Hythe, and the actual seaside. At Hythe, just before the control, I had a puncture. My first on a bike I'd had for eight months and several thousand kilometres. It was a rear puncture, and it took me a while to figure out how to remove the wheel, given the Rohloff gear-changing mechanism which has to be disconnected first, and the fact I'd never done this before. Afterwards it took me a while to work out how to line up the gear into its special slot in the dropouts at the same time as getting the disk of the rear brake to slot between its callipers. But it was warm and sunny, and I was halfway around the course in reasonable time, so it wasn't unpleasant.

The control here was the Light Railway Restaurant at the station on the Hythe and Dymchurch Railway, a railway which for a time boasted the claim of smallest public railway in the world. For those of you not fully aware of the language of trains, *smallest* here refers to the size of the tracks, which here are 12 inches apart. The railway was built in 1925-7 by two racing drivers, one of them killed on the racetrack before it was finished. It runs from Hythe to Dungeness with its original ten steam locomotives engines still running, but also using two antique diesel trains.

The restaurant was nothing special, but it served beans on toast[15], and I also got my second Kent Audax sticker of the day.

During the afternoon I began to feel a little unwell with what a month later I would come to diagnose as heatstroke. For a while I couldn't put my finger on what was up, just that I didn't feel quite right, and my energy was flagging. I'd been cycling on my own since Hythe, although meeting fellow cyclists now and then as I passed them or *vice versa*. Those I passed were generally 20 years older than me.

We followed the line of the coast to Dover, and there picked up Sustrans Route 1 of the National Cycle Network, a path that takes the scenic route from Dover to London, and from there goes on, taking equally scenic routes as it meanders all the way to the Shetland Islands.

A bunch of faster riders caught me a few kilometres before Deal, and I was able to increase my speed to join them, hanging onto somebody's wheel for aerodynamic benefit. The Sustrans route was along the sea front, at times on top of the sea wall, taking the full force of the wind, an amazing place to ride a bike. As we came into Deal and we swapped the sea views for a succession of dull vistas of nondescript housing, I was remembering Deal was one of the original Cinque Ports and wondering what the big deal was. Then the castle made its appearance.

The castle was built in 1539 by Henry VIII, and is a massively solid, low-lying structure in stone stolen from the monasteries he dissolved. Built to withstand artillery, each of the six outer walls curve outwards to deflect cannonballs. Its purpose was to control a strategic point in the sea just offshore called the Downs. Relatively deep, sheltered water, the Downs is protected from inclement weather by the coast to the west and north and from the east by the Goodwin Sands, a sandbar that rises above the waters at low tides.

I had thought I would manage an average of 20km/h, including all stops, and that therefore I would be finished by nine o'clock in the evening, and home by ten, but I was significantly

---

[15] Beans on toast is the perfect cycling food; warming, comforting, and containing plenty of energy, especially carbohydrates. It goes well with tea and is usually the cheapest thing on the menu.

behind that schedule by the time I reached the checkpoint. It had taken me over ten hours to get here, and realistically another hour to reach the 200km mark was likely.

I ate solidly at Deal because I knew I needed to; although I was greatly appreciative of the rest, I was uncharacteristically unenthusiastic about eating.

I passed through Sandwich — a trading centre or *wic* in Old English, which is on sand — and where the local Earl, John Montague, is said to have invented the eponymous snack in the eighteenth century. Although this most famous fun fact is sadly not celebrated by a Museum of Sandwich History or a large statue of the original Fast Food, it is a beautiful town, well worth a visit. From there, the ride cut inland to skip Ramsgate and the Isle of Thanet.

The cramps that had been my constant companion since lunchtime focused themselves into a more acute sensation of being unwell and gave me a powerful urge to find toilet facilities, most likely in the form of a field out of sight of the road. I was convinced it was food poisoning by now, despite a lack of obvious candidates for the poison. The previous time I thought I had food poisoning it turned out to be appendicitis, but now, minus an appendix, that was no longer a possibility. Somewhat reassuringly.

Nevertheless, a brief squat in a field gave me a temporary respite. By this stage I had 100km left to cover. I had no doubt that I would finish, but it was clear I was going to suffer some more.

There was an information control in Birchington. I needed to consult the route sheet to find the right spot, and then I had to be looking for a pub that was behind me. Once there, it took a little investigation to find a sign on the building that admitted it was the Powells Arms. I briefly considered celebrating the existence of the pub, and my finding of it, by stopping for a while, but I wasn't in the mood.

At Herne Bay, I got my stamp and had tea and a teacake at Macari's Coffee Lounge and Ice Cream Parlour. I took a long time eating it, and used the toilet, which was, after all, more civilised than a field. I didn't feel like talking to anyone so I didn't. There was still 78km to go. I texted MGL to warn her I would be later than I had thought.

From Herne Bay it was due west, basically through the Kent Downs towards the start/finish at Meopham, which was a long enough ride into a light headwind punctuated by a few sharp climbs. I wasn't feeling well, but I wasn't feeling any worse than I had for the last few hours. I was needing to make occasional stops at suitable fields, and I ran out of the serviettes I had taken from Macari's and had to improvise using available leaves, but I was making progress. I was going to finish for sure, not least because not finishing presented awkward logistical problems. I couldn't get back to Meopham and the car by public transport, for example.

At Hollingbourne I had to stop for an information control. It was dark now, and therefore reading route sheet or brevet card involved either digging my phone out to use as a torch or struggling to use my bike's front light. Bizarely, I chose the latter. My bike has great lights, but the headlamp is just above the wheel, not the most convenient location for a reading lamp. I also need to take my glasses off to read anything. I was standing astride my bike, gloves and glasses in one hand, brevet card in the other, trying to lean far enough forwards to get the card in the beam of light. The card was now blindingly bright, and it took quite a while of holding this uncomfortable position to read the question I needed to answer. What was the distance to Thurnham? Now all I needed to do was to read the road sign on which I could find the answer, and this required me to put the card back in my pocket and the glasses back on, to lift the bike by the handlebars and turn it to point the headlamp at the road sign. Having accomplished all this, I had forgotten exactly what part of the sign I needed to read. I considered not bothering and asking somebody back at the event headquarters for the necessary information, but now I'd wasted so much time and effort on this activity I was not going to give up. Only once I succeeded I remembered I could have used the camera on my phone. Three miles, anyway. The answer.

The rest of the journey was uneventful. I was cycling on my own, at a gentle pace. My legs were actually tired and I felt faintly nauseous but I had plenty of time in terms of the audax limit and I was gaining a sense of achievement. It was a nice night to be riding. I was happy.

I arrived at Meopham near midnight. The scout hut was ablaze with ugly fluorescent lighting and mostly deserted. Those few people around were one or two semiconscious riders and three or four very tired volunteers. There was little sense of loud celebratory conversation. I called MGL to tell her I had arrived and that I would be home in an hour or so. She told me not to wake her.

CHAPTER FOUR

Porkers

There are relatively few 400km audaxs in the season, for obvious reasons of supply and demand, so there weren't too many options for me. Needing to allow time to get to an event, ride it, get home, and recover sufficiently to be able to cope with classes of excitable teenagers the next day meant I needed to choose an event over a long weekend, or one that happened to occur during a school half term. The choice was more or less between rides in Norfolk, Wales or Dorset, and Dorset is by far the easiest to get to from South West London. I didn't give any thought to what kind of ride it might be, other than to reflect that Dorset is very pretty and it would be fun to cycle there.

As the date approached, I became more apprehensive. Porkers, it turns out, has something of a reputation. There are 5900m of climbing in its 400km[16]. In fact when I asked Shawn Shaw, the organiser, why the ride rejoices in its peculiar name, he told me that it is only the rasher members of the cycling community who take it on. Alternatively, I have heard the name is simply because it is a pig of a ride.

I had suffered in the 300, and although I blamed that very largely on the food poisoning, I did also realise that I might not be fit enough, never having done a 400km ride. Specifically that I might not be fit enough to succeed. In fact I was more worried about this 400km ride than the subsequent planned 600km or indeed the 1200km for PBP. The longer distances are actually a little easier, because, for one thing, the minimum average speed is lower, so there is time to sleep for a while, and that means it is possible to build up a safety margin. Also, I knew I could ride the longer distances, having done two 1200+km rides over the previous two years.

---

[16] Given that on average there is as much downhill as uphill, the climbing must be over a maximum of 200km of actual road, which makes for a minimum average gradient of 3% for the uphills. Of course, there are actually flat bits so the climbing is more concentrated. In some places, as I would find out, very concentrated indeed.

Of course being apprehensive is part of it. If there is no possibility of failure, there is less of a sense of achievement.

The ride started at 2p.m. Never having done a 400, I didn't question this time. It made it easy enough to get to Poole by train without having to get up at stupid o'clock in the morning, and by finishing before 5p.m. the following day, getting home afterwards by public transport would be possible. Apparently the timing also makes it possible to ride the Brevet Cymru ride as well,[17] for those people for whom hard is not hard enough.

The first part of the ride was the gentlest, although it included our first crossing of the Dorset Area of Outstanding Natural Beauty. An AONB is a place that has escaped urbanisation, generally because the landscape is too hilly and too remote for urbanisation to made economic sense, and whose remote, hilly landscape is subsequently recognised as worthy of preservation. Even if it should become less remote or building techniques make it more economically suitable for industry or housing. There was a lot of AONB on this ride, all of it worthy of the name.

At 15km there was an information control. Riders needed to find the name of the first cottage on the right, number 36. It was, and still is, presumably, *Wayside,* unless new occupants have moved in and decided having a name for your house in a row of houses is totally pretentious.

The first twenty kilometres, being the first, invited everyone to pedal flat out, as if their lives depended on it. Rasher members of the cycling community. Even people as old and as sensible as myself were doing it, at least until they began to feel their strength fading.

I found myself riding with Oliver Isles, who commented on the phenomenon of starting too fast. "Every ride I've done recently it's been the same," he said. "I see these guys come flying past me . . ."

I agreed with him wholeheartedly in this, but he went on to say, "and then later on I see those same faces as I pass them when they slow down."

In my experience, the fast boys (and sometimes girls) who pass me early on I never see again. I watched the way he was pedalling — he didn't look like he was having to make much effort, whereas I had already had a meeting with my pain threshold. I asked him if he'd done many events so far this year, by way of small talk. It turned out he had, he really had, he was

---

[17] Another 400km in the hills. This one starts and finishes in Chepstow and includes most of the high ground in South Wales.

aiming to win the AUK AAA Championship. AAA points[18] are given for riding events with significant vertical ascents during the audax year[19]. Most of his points had been accrued through riding a "permanent" 50km route that features a climb of a Cheddar Gorge, a famously steep section of road that winds through a limestone landscape and cheesy tourist town close his home. He was currently leading the AAA competition by a good margin (and did indeed go on to win) and I made a mental note not to waste energy in a fruitless attempt keep up with him.

The Isle of Portland is connected to the mainland of Dorset by the longest sand spit in Europe. A sand spit is a stretch of sand dragged along the coast over the centuries by a prevailing current known to geographers as long shore drift. I remember when I was in the Third Year at school doing a beautiful diagram to show the effect in my geography exercise book, and my dad seeing this for some reason and asking with great concern why I had LSD in bold capitals marked all over the page. In this case, where the Fleet River attempts to join the English Channel, its escape is blocked by this spit, and so the river helps to stretch the sand out to the east until it reaches the once-island of Portland.

The prevailing current basically follows the prevailing westerly winds which on this day were making such a stiff headwind.

The only way onto or off of the island is via Portland Beach Road. This makes the island a perfect place to put a high security prison to augment the other industry here, which is the quarrying of Portland Stone for the eponymous cement.

The beach road is completely flat, and for a short while angled our progress downwind so it was easy going. To make up for that, the road surface was terrible, with wide gaps between concrete sections to make a bone-jarring bump every few metres. Then we reached the island and the road began climbing steeply, going from sea level to 100m in just under a kilometre through the town of Fortuneswell (named after a spring with mystic properties, apparently).

The first control was in front of the Lobster Pot, a restaurant in front of the Portland Bill Lighthouse, where the road runs out. Here Oliver said he was going to bounce, which meant carry straight on once he'd signed in. Having only covered 60km so far. I indicated I was the kind of wimp who needed a tea break after riding for two and a half hours, thinking in any case that I was going to lose his company through an inability to keep up if not by choice. Unfortunately, having got my card stamped and used the loo at the restaurant, I found the Lobster Pot

---

[18] It stands for Audax Altitude Award. See the glossary.

[19] Which runs from October to September, just to be different.

restaurant to be the kind of establishment posh enough not to appear comfortable to a sweaty cyclist, and I decided I too would have to bounce, the difference being my bounce was more like a squash ball than anything more lively. I would be on the lookout for a nearby tea establishment, but this was to prove elusive.

Turning west now, and now on my own, the ride returned me to the beach road by a different route, downhill through the one way system and the urban area of Portland. Then the beach road was again perfectly flat and again poorly surfaced but now had the benefit of a headwind. I gritted my teeth for the next 20km while the unpleasantly busy A354 became the quieter B3136 Chiderell Road before the ride reached the West Dorset Heritage Coast and the hills began, and the wind became much less significant.

Looking at the map, something I didn't actually do before I committed myself to the ride, Porkers is mostly concentrated on those parts of Dorset that are shaded green to indicate their scenic qualities. For scenic read hilly. We bypassed Langton Herring and went through Portsham, following a signpost to Hardy's monument, a 22m tower commemorating Vice Admiral Sir Thomas Hardy, a commander at the Battle of Trafalgar rather than the more famous and equally local Thomas Hardy who wrote books. The tower was just about visible to the right just after I passed the turnoff for it. The route entered The Valley of Stones National Nature Reserve, considered to be one of the finest examples of a Sarsen stone boulder train in Britain. The stones are sandstone blocks that remain from the last ice age. The word Sarcen is a contraction of Saracen, in the middle ages a common term for Muslims, and in the spirit of the unapologetic racism of the age therefore a term for anything freakishly foreign in appearance, like a big lump of unexplained rock in a grassy chalk landscape. Besides the stones, the views were great, and the physical effort required to achieve each view made me appreciate them all the more.

Through the Valley of the Stones to Littlebredy, then Long Bredy and Litton Cheney before passing the 100km mark by the crossroads with the A35. The route headed due north to West Compton and Hoike and then west to Beaminster where the control was at the Coop in the town square. Not having found any tea opportunity since Portland, I stocked up on snacks and bottled sweetened liquid. Then Broadwindsor, Winsham Chard and Combe St Nicholas.

After 157km the route turned north on Station Road out of the delightfully named Hemyock, where for the information control I had to register that the chapel was Baptist. Then Station Road crossed the River Culm into Blackdown, entering the Blackdown Hills AONB on Comb Hill, which took us to over 250m in altitude. We turned east again at Voxmoor and took a slight detour over the M5 to the control at West Buckland at 165km. Hosted by Wellington Wheelers CC, this was a welcoming affair with sufficient quantities of tea and cake to boost morale. It was night by now, and while we had only covered 160km, they were tough kilometres.

After the control, the route returned us to the green part of the map and to the sharp climbs of the Dorset countryside. Riding at night on the stage from West Buckland to Corscombe, we covered the highest elevations and some of the steepest climbs, without being able to see them.

At Corscombe, the village hall was the control, manned, or in fact mostly womanned, by volunteers raising funds for the refurbishment of said hall by selling sandwiches and cakes to weary cyclists in the small hours of the night. As is generally the case with well-meaning good people raising money for charity, in comparison with hard-nosed business people, the cakes and tea were ridiculously cheap. It seems that while out shopping in the High Street, and with a choice of coffee shops, punters are willing to pay upwards of 2 pounds for a beverage, whereas at 3 o'clock in the morning in the only location available for miles around, volunteers feel a thirsty cyclist will resent paying more than 50p for a life-saving brew. Because of this phenomenon it is necessary at such places to eat as much cake as humanly possible (actually that's quite a lot). In fact, on this occasion, I went as far as to stretch out on a thoughtfully provided mat and sleep for an hour, and have more tea and cake on waking before I ventured out in the cold to face more of Dorset's fiercest inclines.

As I was riding now definitively into Sunday morning, the sky gradually brightened to demonstrate that it was a new day, even if I hadn't marked the transition with a decent period of rest. By the time I had come to the information control at Kingston at 244km, it was light enough to identify the lane on the signpost as, would you believe it, Kingston Lane. I made the 47km to West Whitechurch in just over two hours for an early breakfast, despite two big climbs and a handful of short sharp ones. Between the big climbs I passed through the lowland towns of Middlemarsh, Glenville's Wootton, Pleck, and Kings Stag.

At West Whitechurch the stamp on my brevet card said "Merci". After the necessary tea, but without cake, I rejoined the Dorset AONB, climbing over 250m in the process, before descending to relative lowlands through Sterminster Newton. After 40km on this stage, in the village of Hardway, the name perhaps giving a clue to local terrain, it was necessary to note that a signpost to South Brewham gave the distance to that place as 1¼ miles. After this we turned east once more to enter the Cranbourne Chase AONB, and immediately faced the steepest climb of the weekend. The stage came to an end at Cockerton, just south of Warminster. It was coming up to 11am.

From here we travelled more or less parallel to the main A36 Warminster to Salisbury road, only the other side of the River Wylye, reaching the town of Wylye for an information control at 338km, when the cottage on the right at the end of Teapot Street was called Nutmeg. You can't make this up. Here we turned due south for the last 60km down to Poole through the lumpy terrain of the AONB, passing 350km at Sixpenny Handley, then Cranbourne itself, and Wimborne Minster and on towards Poole, where the ride finished at the Café in Hamworthy Park.

I arrived at Poole exhausted and sleep-deprived at a quarter to four on what was something of a grey afternoon. I spent a fair amount of time drinking tea and eating cake and then found my way to the station. I set the alarm on my phone to wake me before the train reached Clapham Junction where I needed to change, and had no difficulty falling asleep.

CHAPTER FIVE

The Bryan Chapman Memorial 600km

I had been looking forward to this ride for a while. I had looked into it in 2013 as preparation for riding LEL but hadn't been able to do it then because it fell within term time.

This year, by good fortune, the Bryan Chapman fell at the beginning of my school's half term break. I booked my place early. The notes on the Audax UK website stated it was possible to camp at the start before the event, which suited me. The wording "it is possible" sounded a little ambiguous, implying something less than, for example, "You're very welcome to camp". *It is possible* could in fact mean *you are not welcome to camp, in fact it is against the law, but people have got away with it in the past.* I figured I could worry about that later.

For this 600, I thought I would carry the same amount of stuff as I intended to for PBP. In addition, for the night's camping, I would take a pannier bag with a bivvy bag and sleeping bag which I could afterwards leave at the event headquarters. Luxury. For the train journey I allowed myself a pair of non-cycling trousers for my own comfort and to spare fellow passengers the trauma of seeing a man in tights.

Yes, the train! Chepstow is easy enough to get to by rail, and if I was going to camp there beforehand I didn't need to travel at a time when public transport was still asleep.

I took the train on the Friday night, cycling to Paddington station from my house. I had recently discovered the GPS navigation app Pocket Earth[20] and intended to use my phone as a GPS unit for the first time, installing it on the handlebars with a sturdy clamp and waterproof

---

[20] PocketEarth.com I will happily recommend, and perhaps as a reward, the developers will upgrade me to a premium account. It's totally free, using open source mapping which you can download onto your phone. This means you don't need a phone signal to see where you are, just the signals from GPS satellites. The only problem is that using a smart phone as a GPS unit is fairly demanding on the phone battery, and a ride of more than a few hours is not possible without being able to recharge the phone.

housing.[21] I needed full use of it to find my way.

I arrived at Newport at about 9p.m. to face the 25km to Chepstow along Sustrans National Cycle Route 4. It was possible to get to Chepstow by train, but it involved a change and some waiting around. Cycling the last part seemed the better option. I had also considered cycling from Bristol which was also perfectly feasible and had the added bonus of cycling over the Severn Bridge, one of them anyway, but it added too many miles.

It was a pleasant but uneventful ride along the empty A48. I arrived at the race headquarters after dark, and found it uninspiring, a community centre at the end of a cul de sac. It was brick built, 1970s I guessed, like the houses around it, and deathly quiet. Everything was locked up. There was no sign of life other than a couple of parked cars and the glare of street lamps. On close inspection, however, one of the cars had a rack for carrying bicycles, which was reassuring.

I couldn't see any sign of camping going on. The only space to camp was a strip of grass around the edge of the car park, brilliantly illuminated by the street lights. I didn't need much space, and the grass looked comfortable, but I didn't think I was going to get much in the way of sleep under the light. Nevertheless, I locked my bike to the lamppost, the only benefit it was giving me.

Only after I'd done this did I notice that the high fence at the edge of the car park had a gate. I wandered across and found this gate unlocked. Behind it was a field of mown grass.

The field was in pitch darkness away from the light of the car park. I imagined there might be fellow audaxers camping there, but I could see no sign of them. It was 10:30 and I had little desire to go searching.

I parked the bike by the fence on the car park side and locked it there. I had a good lock with me for this purpose, knowing I didn't need to carry it with me on the ride. I carried my camping stuff around to the other side of the fence and shook out the bivvy bag. I wanted the bike on the car park side because I had an advertisement for my first book attached to the saddlebag and I wanted people to see it.

Now I had to find the bivvy bag that needed to be unrolled, the sleeping mat that needed to be inflated, and the sleeping bag that needed to be pushed into the bivvy bag. Finally I could

---

[21] I use Quad Lock, which uses its own phone case. I leave the case on my phone all the time — it does a good job of protecting it from the frequent drops I subject it to. It's expensive but not extravagantly so, very convenient, and very secure. As you can read in chapter fifteen, I have crash-tested this product.

remove the non-cycling trousers and crawl inside my sleeping bag. After this, full of adrenaline and wide awake, I tried to get to sleep.

Sleep did take a while to happen, but it happened, and I got several precious hours in before cars started arriving at silly o'clock in the morning and I reconsidered the wisdom of being so close to the car park. In daylight, when I sat up, I could see the grounds of the community centre were huge, and there were half a dozen tents at the other side of it, where their inhabitants could enjoy a good hour's extra undisturbed sleep.

People who arrived early that morning presumably did so because they drove long distances to get here and they allowed themselves a decent margin of error. They then needed to remove the bikes from bike racks and fettle them a little, and fettle themselves as well, and then chat amicably and energetically amongst themselves while they waited for the event headquarters to open, which it did at 6 a.m. I was aware that sleep would be in very short supply during the ride and tried to get another hour of it, and had at least partial success.

The fence I was lying down beside was a focus for people to lean a bike, and the advertisement on my saddlebag attracted some attention, which is the point of any advertisement, and at least one person bought my book on Kindle there and then, which I thought was a good way to start the day.

However unwelcome the thought of sleeping in a bivvy bag might appear, it is so very comfortable once you are in it and there is a chilly morning outside. Eventually however, it was time to move. I changed into the necessary Lycra inside my bivvy bag. Once I was up, it took less than a minute to roll bivvy, mat, and sleeping bag up together and stuff them into the pannier. Then I went inside for breakfast.

Consuming the necessary calories and liquid was made more difficult by the fact that immediately I began meeting people I knew from previous audaxes, including Alastair in his trademark pristine Dulwich Paragon attire. I covered a large part of LEL with Alastair, who is of course now world-famous as a character in my first book. I hadn't seen him in the 18 months since, so there was plenty to catch up on. Nevertheless, through sheer force of will I managed to consume sandwiches, cake and toast enough I thought I would survive the first 50km.

For many audaxers, The Bryan Chapman is the highlight of the season. Such have I learned from the forums. It is a physically demanding ride, with over 8000m of climbing in its 600km (an average gradient of 1.3% by my previous method) and it passes along some of the most scenic Welsh roads to do it.

The route itself is straightforward. Start at Chepstow near the south coast of the principality, then ride north by way of the west coast at Barmouth to reach the north coast and cross the bridge to Anglesey. Coast to coast to coast. And then come back more or less the same way. But with a diversion along the border with England.

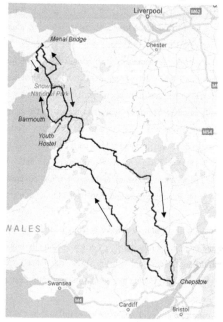

Soon enough the preliminaries were over and I was heading for North Wales on a pleasant sunny morning. In contrast to the Porkers 400 there seemed to be a sufficient number of cyclists setting off at a reasonable pace, so I wasn't forced into an adrenaline-fuelled racing start.

Having the advert on the back of the saddlebag initiated conversations, especially in combination with my souvenir LEL 2013 jersey. These conversations generally went something like this:

"What's that sign on the back of your bike? I can't really read it."

"That's my advert. I wrote a book."

"What's it about?"

"Well…" And I would do my sales pitch.

The dialogue generally continued one of three ways:

a) "That's really interesting. I rode LEL last time as well/I'm definitely thinking about doing LEL and going to buy your book."

b) "That's really interesting. I might read it." Which I know means they won't, and that's forgivable, and they're being polite about it, which is good.

c) "Hey I've read that! I really enjoyed it."

The last category gave me a lot of pleasure.

After a couple of hours I found myself talking to a man in his mid 30s about LEL, which he had also ridden. After a few minutes of conversation he wondered if we'd met, and at this suggestion, I realised we had.

"Did you take deodorant with you?" I asked.

"You wrote the book!" (*The* book, please note.)

Which he'd clearly read. He'd been amazed to find himself in its pages admitting to the deodorant. And to have read my take on the people and places he'd encountered two years earlier. (He was MAN1 in that book. We introduced ourselves properly now, but of course I forgot his name. Next time we meet I will write it down.)

"I was jealous of you because you got to ride with that really beautiful Italian girl."

The reason I wrote *Virgin*, and why I'm writing this, when I usually write serious but as yet unpublished novels, was that I knew there was a small but niche market for it. Very niche. At this time, only a few months after its publication, fewer than 500 people had bought *Virgin*[22], but a good number of those were the kind of people who would ride the Bryan Chapman.

The Bryan Chapman has the simplest of routes, as I said, and the route sheet, for all its 600km, is shorter than those of many 200km events. There aren't many roads over much of the terrain, which is what keeps the directions simple.

It includes 8200m of climbing, accounting for eight AAA points. This vertical distance is not quite the height of Everest, but is significantly more than the distance you'd climb to reach that peak starting from Kathmandu. I mention this because there is a cycling cult of Everesting with its own website.[23] The rules for Everesting are basically that you ride repeatedly up and down the same hill, by the same route — one of the bureaucracy of minor rules

---

[22] At the time of writing, 2500 people have bought, if not read, my first publication. I am well on the way to becoming a millionaire.

[23] http://www.everesting.cc

designed to avoid what they call kinetic gain — until you complete 8848m of climbing. The Bryan Chapman wouldn't count, even if there were another 650m, as it certainly isn't one climb repeated, and for me at least, included a sleep stop.

The Bryan Chapman has amazing scenery, but unlike Porkers, there are no really steep gradients. The hills are long rather than sharp, raising the riders up to high, desolate moorland, and to outrageous views.

After just under three hours we were through the Brecon Beacons National Park and just beyond its borders was the first control, in the village of Bronllys. Bronllys is a small village of less than a thousand inhabitants, but it nonetheless boasts a hospital, a twelfth century motte-and-bailey castle, a leisure centre, and a post office, as well as the Honey Café which served as the first control.

There was nobody here to stamp a brevet card, so a receipt was called for. So was a cup of tea.

From here we continued along the A479 and then the A470. I met up with Alastair on the road and we talked more about what we'd been doing in the year and more since LEL. We'd been in touch since, via the yacf website mostly. I had sent him a pre-publication electronic copy of my book[24], and he put a nice review on Amazon when it came out. Alastair got to see my sales pitch at work several times during the day.

We met a team of five Rapha employees who were riding Bryan Chapman instead of a day at work, and who would naturally feature in promotional literature with decent photographs.[25] Alastair spoke to one girl, saying, "I really like your shoes," which I thought was a pretty dubious chat up line until I noticed she was wearing bright blue soft Italian leather cycling shoes, and subsequent conversation revealed Alastair really did like these shoes the same colour as his cycling kit, although the price would put off anyone who wasn't either a Rapha employee with a discount, or a millionaire.

It was a warm and sunny day and the wind was light and anyway mostly at our backs. I chatted to Alastair and the hours went by.

At Llagurig, we turned west on the A44. Llagurig is a town on the River Wye with about 700 people which almost had a railway service during the Victorian era. Around 1860 both the Manchester and Milford Railway and the Mid-Wales Railway companies were licensed by parliament to build a railway through the same region. Competition between these companies

---

[24] I promise to stop footnoting product placements if you commit to buying it.

[25] http://pages.rapha.cc/stories/bryand-the-bryan-chapman-memorial-2015

and a financial downturn led to the Llagurig branch line being abandoned as soon as it was finished, but not before a single goods train belonging to the Mid-Wales Railway completed the route, thus marking the line as open and requiring the Manchester and Milford Railway to pay part of the cost of the now useless station in Llagurig. We followed the A44 most of the way to Aberystwyth but turned north at Capel Bangor, eventually joining the A487.

The second control was situated in the village of Tre'r Ddôl. I bought sandwiches and bananas and a decent cup of coffee at the *Siop Cynfelin* (community shop) and put the receipt carefully with my brevet card as evidence.

After food and coffee, I met a young woman who'd just arrived and was admiring my bike outside the shop. It turned out she also has a bike made by Ryan, although she wasn't riding it this weekend, and we chatted about Ryan and good bike design and she urged me to get in touch with him to say how happy I am with the bike (something I still haven't done). Five minutes later when I was back on the road with Alastair, I realised that I'd been talking to Emily Chappell, a cycle courier, explorer, and blogger whose attempt to ride around the world I had followed avidly. I recommend her blog and her book, *What Goes Around.*[26]

The afternoon rolled on, and we rolled with it, up long, long gentle climbs and then down again. It was a beautiful day. The weather forecast for Sunday was bleak, so it made sense to enjoy the moment.

Other than this, there was next to nothing to delay us, and we continued north until the road reunited us with the A470 at a T-junction and we turned left and east to Dolgellau, following the River Wnion towards the sea. We didn't cross the bridge to reach Dolgellau itself, a town whose history boasts Celts who refused to be conquered by the Romans, a Quaker settlement, and a minor gold rush. Instead we cycled on 6km, then did a U-turn when I realised my navigation was faulty, and took the minor road uphill to Kings Youth Hostel. The hostel was booked for the weekend by organiser Richie Tout, and it served as a control going both north and south, with both food and beds available.

I doubted many would be ready for a kip after 225km, but the distance on the way back seemed about right at just under 400km. The approach to the Youth Hostel I'd been told was the steepest climb of the whole route, and so it proved. Under thick forest cover, the damp road wound its way upwards, parts of it one in five or worse. Ahead of us there was a rider walking, which was an indication of how hard it was. On close inspection this man was running, bike

---

[26] I hope plugging somebody else's book makes up for all that shameless plugging of my own. Her blog is at http://thatemilychappell.com

over his shoulders like somebody in a cyclocross event. I thought how odd it was for somebody unable to peddle their way up a climb to have energy enough to run, but quickly realised the bike was an orange fixie I'd seen unloaded from a car in front of my bivvy bag that morning, and the man running confirmed my idea that you had to be hard to ride this kind of event without gears.

At the Youth Hostel I met Richie Tout who was presiding over the control with the help of his teenage daughter. The daughter was doing English homework in between stamping cards. I also met Simon, whom I'd first met on the Scottish Highlands ride.[27] Simon was talking about a plan to avoid the incoming bad weather.

"The rain is coming from the North, right?" he said. "So all we have to do is outrun it."

The simple way to accomplish this was to ride through the night. Storms were due in Anglesey around midnight and would travel south at a cyclist's speed, more or less. Any rider moving southwards from there would stay dry as long as they didn't stop. It sounded a reasonable plan, but then many other things can be accomplished if you don't need to sleep, and at the time I was well aware, after less than a full night's rest on Friday, and 225km already today, that I would rather sleep and then get wet than be dry and sleep-deprived.

When Emily Chappell arrived, I spoke to her again, telling her I was a fan, which turned out to be something of a conversation stopper, and I felt embarrassingly starstruck. I met Bob Geldof once at a parents' evening and did much better, probably because I was acting in a professional capacity. I didn't let on I know all the words to I Don't Like Mondays.

From the Youth Hostel we returned to the main A470 and turned left to continue eastwards, passing through Arthog, a village where the entrepreneur Solomon Andrews started to build a holiday resort but stopped after six houses at Mawddach Crescent. Andrews found the land unsuitable, so these six luxurious large houses sit like follies with a beautiful view of the Mawddach estuary. My parents have a friend who owns a flat in one of them, and MGL and I once spent a weekend with them here when Junior was seven. I remember he christened our new car by throwing up in the back just before we arrived, poor boy.

We passed Mawddach Crescent and Arthog and continued down for a few kilometres before turning off onto the Mawddach Trail cycle path, which follows the route of the old GWR

---

[27] In fact after that event I'd stayed the night with him at his mother's house a few miles up the coast from the finish, after being bitten by his uncle's dog. Long story.

Ruabon-Barmouth railway line, which once went from the resort town of Barmouth to Bala and Dolgellau. Now the cycle path took us over the footbridge to Barmouth.

Barmouth, at the mouth of the river Mawddach, is so named because of a sand bar that makes navigation treacherous. In Welsh, it is *Abermaw*, from *aber*, meaning river mouth, and the river's name. And it is a really lovely town. William Wordsworth, who visited often, thought so, and wrote, "With a fine sea view in front, the mountains behind, the glorious estuary running eight miles inland, and Cadair Idris within compass of a day's walk, Barmouth can always hold its own against any rival." I would have liked to stay there for an hour or two, but you don't get to cover 600km in a weekend by dilly-dallying for an hour or two in nice places, so I contented myself to wistful looks to left and right as I passed through.

We rode up the coast to Harlech, where the malevolent looking castle could be seen between houses. The name 'Harlech' is from either the Welsh *ardd* meaning high or *hardd* meaning fair, and *llech* meaning rock. The castle was built in 1283 by Edward I as part of his campaign to conquer the country. A wholly military establishment, it was a key focus in subsequent Welsh uprisings and in the War of the Roses. Originally built next to the sea, it is now about half a mile inland, atop high, fair cliffs.

From here, deeper into Snowdonia, is some of the most beautiful wilderness in the UK. Snowdonia was the third designated National Park in Britain in 1951, after the Lake and Peak Districts. In Welsh it is *Eryri*, which probably originally meant Highlands.

We cycled up the awesome Glaslyn gorge, where the river tears its way down between steep wooded hills, to the tourist town of Beddgelert, which is apparently named after a heroic dog called Gelert. The dog belonged to Llywelyn the Great, Prince of Gwynedd, and the story goes like this: Llywelyn returned from hunting to find his baby son missing, the cradle tipped over, and the dog with blood all over its mouth. Thinking that his dog had killed the baby, Llywelyn without further thought drew his sword and hacked it to death. In response to the dog's death cries, the baby also cried, and Llywelyn found him under the cradle together with the wolf Gelert had killed to protect the child. Naturally enough Llywelyn was then overcome with remorse. He gave the dog a splendid funeral and never smiled again. *Bedd* means grave. None of this is true, sadly, despite there being a statue of the dog. Beddgelert is almost certainly named as the burial site of a seventh century saint, Gelert (a.k.a. Celer, Celert or Kellarth). The dog story is probably the initiative of an innkeeper in the 1790s. But stories don't need to be true to be interesting.[28]

I dropped Alastair on one of the climbs as we rode into the evening, I can't remember where, and joined a couple of younger guys wearing Audax Club Hackney hats and beards.[29] I'm quite good at cycling uphill, since I weigh about 9½ stone (or 60kg) dripping wet. When the roads were flat, I could keep up with the ACH lot by hanging onto their wheels.

It was now cooling off, but the warm day had had its effect. I was feeling unwell once again. By now I was pretty sure that the sickness I had been suffering from on long rides was heatstroke, and now resolved to make greater efforts to keep myself hydrated, but this resolution, which was to serve me well through the rest of the year, was no benefit to me now. I wasn't feeling at all good and was pretty sure it was going to get worse.

We rode past Llyn Gwynant, a glacial lake about 50 hectares in size, popular for canoeing and kayaking and used as a filming location in the 2003 film 'Lara Croft Tomb Raider: The Cradle of Life'. From the lake there was a long climb, where I kept up with other cyclists by following them closely through the wind and being literally a lightweight on the climbs, and then we came to the town of Llanberis.

Llanberis grew up around the slate quarrying industry, but since the closure of quarries in the 1930s, the main industry has been tourism. There is also the Dinorwig Power Station, which is like a giant battery made of water — water is pumped to a high reservoir when there is surplus capacity, and then allowed to run back through generators when there is high demand. Sometimes I tell children about this in science lessons. The ruins of Dolbadarn Castle, which were famously painted by Richard Wilson and J.M.W. Turner, stand above the village. The thirteenth century fortress was built by Llywelyn the Great. According to the United Kingdom Census, the population of Llanberis is about 2000, and 81% of them population speak Welsh fluently. From there it was about 20km to the Menai Suspension Bridge.

---

[28] The story occurs all over the world with different variations, the wolf being sometimes a snake or tiger, and the dog at times a mongoose, or a bear, and also turns up in the Disney movie *The Lady and the Tramp* (this time without the tragedy).

[29] You can join Audax Club Hackney simply by asking to. You can buy a hat for £5. None of its members apparently come from that inner-city borough, but they all look as if they could do. A certain air of streetwise hardness is part of it. And beards.

The Bridge (*Pont Grog y Borth* in Welsh) connects the island of Anglesey with the mainland of Wales, and is "the first important modern suspension bridge" according to Encyclopaedia Britannia. It spans 176 metres over the dangerous waters of the Menai Strait. The high banks and fast flowing waters of the Strait would have made it difficult to build piers on the shifting sands of the sea-bed, so the two carriageways were suspended by iron chains from towers at either end. The bridge was designed by Thomas Telford and completed in 1826.

Before this bridge, cattle from Anglesey used to be driven into the water and made to swim across the Strait to get them to the mainland and to markets, a not-surprisingly dangerous practice which often resulted in the loss of valuable animals.

The day after the end of the First World War, 12 November 1918, Air Marshal Sir Thomas Elmhirst flew airship SSZ73 under the bridge, which must have been something to see.

It was night by the time we got there. I stopped for a couple of minutes to take photographs, but quickly decided it was too cold to compose anything more than a snapshot. Then I got back on the bike and cycled over it to the island of Anglesey and the town that was once called Porthaethwy and is now simply Menai Bridge. I followed tail lights to the control, turning back on myself at the roundabout at the end of the bridge, and taking a steep little descent to the Scout hut practically underneath the bridge itself.

It was 9:45 and I was five hours ahead of schedule. I used some of that time in eating and drinking tea. I considered finding a patch of floor for sleeping, and in retrospect that would have been the best idea, but for some reason I did not. Whether because I thought it was still too early, whether it was the idea that the 82km back to the Youth Hostel would not take so long, or whether, at a subconscious level, I had taken on board Simon's plan to avoid the storm, I don't know, but I was back on the road after just over half an hour.

It was a lovely warm night, and with tea and food inside me I felt a lot better. The beautiful scenery was less beguiling by night, but still there, and the wind that would later bring all that rain was going the right way, and so it was at least half an hour before I started to feel wretched again.

41

The route had us backtracking to the Llanberis road but keeping on in the direction of Canaervon for ten kilometres before turning off on the A4087 to Beddgelert via Llyn (Lake) Cwellyn, which was basically invisible in the darkness.

But now I had started to suffer properly. At one point I had to excuse myself in the middle of a sales pitch for an impromptu squat behind convenient rocks, and I was not unhappy to see the small group of riders I'd been riding with disappear up the road, becoming nothing more than a collection of red lamps dancing away from me, gradually fading from sight. I wouldn't have been able to keep up with them for very long anyway. I didn't feel like talking to anyone, and I didn't want to keep explaining why I needed to get off my bike and hide behind a rock or a tree.

It wasn't my first squat of the evening. I was needing to stop every half hour or so, and at the same time feeling less and less like an athlete, or even like a human being.

Eventually Alastair caught up with me. I think he was riding with other people, but he let them ride on to keep me company. I think he was surprised that others had left me behind. In any case he reduced his pace and rode with me though the rest of the night, waiting for me numerous times while I was forced to stop in the dark.

People die of diarrhoea. When I was a kid it was something embarrassing and inconvenient, and I was amazed to later learn it kills over a million people a year, mostly under fives. It wasn't until an episode of food poisoning in Morocco that I truly understood how it could be fatal. What I was feeling now wasn't going to kill me, and I wasn't going to let it finish my ride, but there were moments when being dead felt like an option.

I had thoughtfully provided myself with a sheaf of napkins at the last café I'd visited, but these had long gone by the small hours, and I had been improvising with foliage as best I could ever since. By this time I was feeling lightheaded from tiredness, with more than 350km already accomplished, from lack of sleep, and from being unwell. I was struggling to stay awake, and had it been warm enough I would have found a place to lie down for a couple of hours. It was like being drunk, but without any of the pleasurable bits.

I was wearing gloves. The good thing about wearing gloves while grabbing useful plant matter in the dark is that if you chance upon something sharp you don't hurt your hands. The bad thing is that by not hurting your hands you don't realise when you have picked up something less than comfortable to use.

Which is how I came to wipe my bum with a handful of stinging nettles.

It is quite an experience, let me tell you. I may have shouted something. I went from semiconscious to wide awake in the time it takes for nerve impulses to reach the brain. The sensation was acute, and quite frankly, surprising. And I have rarely felt so alive.

"Are you all right?" Alastair asked.

"Er . . . Yeah."

With my eyes watering, I retrieved my bike and got back onto the road, pedalling with a significantly greater tempo than hitherto. The pain was no worse for sitting on it, nor any better, but it definitely kept me awake very effectively, and distracted me from any previous symptoms. Either by luck or by direct causation, I had no further need of al fresco toilet facilities on that ride.

In the dark we passed through Beddgelert, rejoining the northward route for a while, then at Penrhyndeudraeth turning inland on the A420, taking the more direct route to Dolgellau. It was of little interest to me at the time, but Penrhyndeudraeth means peninsula with two beaches: the lower half of the town used to be a lake, which was then drained to create the area where the High Street is today. The names of terraces in Penrhyndeudraeth, such as Glanllyn ("lakeside") and Penllyn ("end of the lake"), refer to a time when the site was underwater. Fascinating.

To give an idea of the quality intellectual conversations you might have while cycling through the night, I might tell you we spent some time discussing the shadow Alastair's new front light made on the road in front of him. I told Alastair I felt threatened by it. Whether or not it is apparent from the picture, this shadow had the shape of a particularly large and erect penis, whereas the shadow of my own, similar mudguard and broadly similar headlamp suggested no such thing.

We arrived at the Youth Hostel just before four in the morning. Alastair thought he would snatch an hour or two of sleep and be off again. I told him not to bother waking me. I was really grateful to him for keeping me company during the night, and knew I would be okay the next day, but I wanted a decent night's sleep first.

I was conscious of needing a shower, and did that, changing into a new pair of Lycra shorts and vest, and then I crawled into a warm bed somebody had very recently climbed out of. I was asleep more or less instantly.

A decent night's sleep is relative. Three hours later, at 7:30, and feeling significantly better, I was having breakfast. Simon was there at the same time. I asked him about his plan not to stop, and he admitted how good an idea it had seemed at the time. It was wet outside, the promised weather not letting us down.

Outside, I pulled my garish yellow waterproofs out of my saddlebag. As I was setting off, I saw Simon fiddling with his bike and asked him what was wrong with it.

"Nothing wrong with the bike. It's me not fit enough to ride it."

I saw he was riding fixed, and he explained he was flipping the rear wheel over to give him a lower gear, since he didn't have the strength to push the higher one over the roads to come.

"You're doing pretty well to be riding fixed here at all," I said.

He told me he was determined to ride PBP on fixed, and thought it was only appropriate to do the qualifying events on fixed as well.

"Good luck with that."

I set off into the falling mist.

I was tired from lack of sleep, and I felt weak from having been ill, but I was very happy that the torment in my guts had disappeared and I was no longer lightheaded and nauseous. The land was brutal and bleak, the clouds came all the way down to meet it, and the rain was relentless, but it was warm enough, and the steady climb during the first hour meant I would stay warm. It was good to be on the road. I was totally on my own, a figure in silly yellow Gore-Tex gently plodding up a hill in the rain. I guess I like cycling.

A couple of hours later the rain dried up and the sun came out. I passed riders from time to time, greeting them warmly and riding alongside for a short while before I needed to move on, uncomfortable at their pace. And then I could see a couple of riders in the distance in front of me who remained there, half a mile away and getting closer only gradually, so I was clearly not moving much faster. Egged on by the sight of them up the road, I was motivated to speed up for somebody to talk to.

And so I met Tym and Jessica. They were good company, and it was good to have people to share the scenery with.

We reached the control at the community centre in Aberhafesp at 11:18, ready for a second breakfast, or brunch, or early lunch, or whatever you'd call it as long as it was food. With tea. Fortunately there was lots of it available. Then onwards and in good spirits. There was only 140km to go.

Actually 160km, my new companions informed me. Although this was a 600km event, it was actually 619km in physical length. Tym informed me that as far as the Audax Club Parisien was concerned, those extra 19km did not exist. You had to accomplish the 619km in 40 hours to average the $600/40 = 15$ km/h required average speed. If a rider finished at a 11:15 tonight, having ridden 619km at 15 km/h in 41 hours and 16 minutes, they would not be able to use this audax as a qualifier. Neither Tym nor Jessica were planning on doing PBP, but it was good they knew this anyway.

Both of them had done rides of this length or longer, so naturally they were subjected to my sales pitch. In fact Jessica, either from genuine interest, or kindness, or a desire to get this annoying man to just shut up very quickly, declared she would buy a copy as soon as she was home.

I was feeling much better, but well aware that any good feeling would disappear if I tried to push the pace a little, so I didn't mind waiting at the top of climbs for a few moments. I was glad of company and, despite the arbitrary unfairness of 19 extra kilometres that didn't even

45

count, I calculated that our current pace would bring us to the finish at Chepstow with a comfortable margin.

The route took us over the highest climb of the weekend, at 468m, on the way to the border with England. We followed the edge of the Shropshire Hills AONB, following the border for 25km, before we crossed into England and Herefordshire. The first village in England was Brampton Bryan, which boasts some lovely thatched cottages, the ruins of a castle destroyed during the English Civil War in 1644, and a truly remarkable and ancient yew hedge, a single and continuous hedge that lines just about every street.

The road took us south through pretty but relatively undemanding roads in the sunshine. We stopped at Weobly, where the control was the One Stop Shop, and the one stop included the purchase of both ice cream and suncream. We sat in a very thoughtfully-provided green area of park benches and shady trees. Mark Rigby, who'd organised the Highlands and Islands event the previous year, and was working as a volunteer on this one, took a break from patrolling the route on his motorbike to join us for the ice cream, but not the suncream.

We re-entered Wales, riding into Monmouthshire and, indeed, Monmouth, and then followed the River Wye southwards, passing the ruins of Tinturn Abbey that have inspired a long list of poets and painters. We approached Chepstow with the 600km already achieved, and enjoyed a good view of the two Severn bridges. The one nearer to us, the original Severn Bridge, was opened in 1966 and extended the M4 motorway into Wales. The second one, further to the south, and called, imaginatively, the Second Severn Crossing, was built 30 years later and took the M4 with it.[30]

We arrived back at the community centre HQ a little before 8 o'clock in the evening, with the sun still shining, and I had my card stamped with a zebra. There was tea and cake and conversation, pain and kindness and elation, the body rewarding the completion of the arbitrary and arduous task with a rush of pleasurable hormones.

Tym and Jessica wondered how I would get home, there being a peculiar lack of trains crossing the bridge on a Sunday evening. I told them I could always cycle to Bristol and catch a London train from there, trying to make it sound like this would be a pleasurable, or at least a not overly unpleasurable, thing to do. Further investigation showed that even those travel arrangements didn't work out, and I would basically have to wait until about 5am on Monday for a London train, whether I waited in Chepstow or in Bristol. At least I had a bivvy bag, but

---

[30] The original Severn Bridge, now demoted, carries the M48 instead.

I was pleased when they offered me a lift to Swindon, where they lived, and their floor to sleep on.

It took a while for them to find their car, a small hatchback, safely parked in a nearby side street, and somewhat longer to fit three bicycles into the rear of it while still leaving enough space for a passenger. Once this was achieved, I was polite enough not to fall asleep on the journey.

Tym and Jessica had only recently moved into their house, and it was still mostly decorated with half-unpacked boxes. Lots of the boxes contained cycling equipment or had done once. They clearly shared an interest. The new home-owners assured me that the centre of Swindon was actually a nice place, despite what everybody said, and I admit that so it proved. They lived just around the corner from the station, in a house originally built for railway construction workers.

I found a space between boxes in their spare room and, after rolling out my sleeping bag and climbing in, I had a few moments to notice how uncomfortable the floor was before I passed out.

Next morning I was treated to excellent coffee and scrambled eggs before I had to face the 200 metre ride to the station.

CHAPTER SIX

Two Double Ds

The Ditchling Devil

In early June I did the Ditchling Devil 200km audax ride organised by Willesden Cycling Club. This event has as its unique selling point that it starts within a couple of miles of my house, and it was the first ever audax I attempted, back in 2012. It is basically a ride from London to Brighton and back, with the advantage of starting further out of London than Clapham Common and of having far, far fewer than 27 000 riders, so it is possible to use the lovely country lanes the British Heart Foundation London to Brighton ride once used, before its sheer size forced it to use wider roads closed to traffic. The name comes from its use of the Ditchling Beacon going towards Brighton —the climb made famous by the suffering there of so many casual cyclists as they approach their ultimate destination — and of the Devils Dyke Road on the way back.

London to Brighton is a famous journey, famed for vintage car rallies, for journeys by thousands of Mods on their scooters and Rockers on their motorbikes in the 1960s, and for cycle events and records from the days of the first bicycles. In 1893 Miss Tessie Reynolds, then 16 years old, rode one of the new safety bicycles from Brighton, where she lived, to Londonand back in 8½ hours[31]. She wore "pantaloons", great voluminous garments which covered her from ankle to neck but allowed for more movement than the traditional Victorian lady's skirts. This "rational" dress was nevertheless heavily criticised by (male) cyclists, particularly in Cyclist magazine, but her achievement was naturally celebrated among the suffragette movement.

---

[31] The turning point was either Hyde Park Corner or London Bridge. Both have been reported. Perhaps she visited both, just to be sure.

With her clothing still more restrictive than modern Lycra, and her bike a heavyweight by to-day's standards, her achievement is all the more impressive, and it was a record that stood for a year before it was broken by a man.[32]

I took ten hours to do the Ditchling Devil in 2015. To be fair to me this ride is longer than Miss Reynolds's, and rather hillier than a route between London and Brighton needs to be. Crossing the South Downs cannot be avoided, and Ditchling Beacon and especially Devils Dyke are no steeper or harder than alternative routes, but there is no need to return via the Surrey Hills.

The ride is popular not simply because of its convenient start and finish point, although there is a shortage of audax rides so conveniently close to London, but also its quickly estab-lished reputation as one of the best organised audax events on the calendar.

Perhaps inspired by Simon, perhaps feeling strong after Porkers and the Bryan Chapman, I decided I would do this on my fixed wheel bike. I suspected I would have to walk on one or two slopes in the North Downs on the way home, but otherwise I knew it would be manageable. Besides it was only 200km.

Because the Ditchling Devil starts so close to my home, every year I have done it I have arrived slightly late.[33] Arriving slightly late for an audax start normally means you have to ride without the benefits of companionship, without the aerodynamic advantage of having help pushing through the air, and not least, without help in navigation. With a large enough group of cyclists, somebody will actually *know* the way. For the Ditchling Devil, arriving late was fortunately not so much of a problem as the ride is popular enough it took a good 15 minutes for all the cyclists to make their way out of the car park at Wimbledon Common. I managed to grab a doughnut as I signed on and still set off with a group.

With plenty of other cyclists going pretty much flat out, perhaps as a desire to catch those who had managed to start the event at 8 AM, I made very rapid progress following wheels towards Brighton, reaching the first control for tea and a (vegetarian) "all-day breakfast in a bun" in a layby at about 50km, and reaching Ditchling Beacon around 11 o'clock. It was some-thing of a grunt to get to the top in the fixed gear, especially as the bicycle and car traffic was enough to make any weaving across the road in search of shallower incline impossible. Never-theless, few people managed to pass me going up the hill, and when I reached the top I had

---

[32] Mr E White of Dover Road Club.

[33] The theory is that if you have only a short distance to travel, then if you are a little late setting off, you have far less chance to make up the time before you arrive. A tardiness of five minutes might be minor for a one-hour journey, but for a ten minute one it is fatal.

something left. I wouldn't have stopped if not for the need to record the word written on an Audax UK Notice.

That word was *OYTT*, which, as many people observed, is not a word in any ordinary sense. Totally inexplicable, but very clearly written in bold capitals, so I dutifully made a note of it.

From there, the road is level for a long way, then dips slightly for a long shallow descent before it reaches the main A27 dual carriageway, which requires a little perseverance to cross. There, Ditchling Road descends steeply towards Brighton, and then the route turns sharply right, off the main road into town and sharply upwards through a housing estate before it emerges from its urban environment on the road to Devils Dyke. After a steep enough climb, there is a long gradual uphill towards the Devils Dyke National Trust site and car park, where the second information control was another non-word on an Audax UK banner, this time *GOTG*.

At this point I overheard somebody saying the words of the day were acronyms of *One Year Time Trial* and *Go On Teethgrinder*, in honour of Steve Abraham's efforts.

Onwards. From there, a short 10km to Upper Beading and the wonderful garden party that was the control, at the organiser's house, where I found some shade under one of many gazebos to dispatch a plate of pasta and a bowl of peaches and Ambrosia creamed rice. Perhaps the only thing missing was a glass of champagne.

The next 40km were relatively gentle and brought me to the final control at the sports pavilion in Chiddingfold. There was tea and cake and I got an octopus stamped on my brevet card. It was a lovely day and the prevailing wind was at my back.

After that, the North Downs were the thing to look forward to, the only real barrier between myself and the comforts of home. While the Surrey Hills are not the Alps or even the Brecon Beacons, they are hard enough, and the climbs are significantly steeper than those other places. After 170km the roads are steeper still, Combe Lane near the village of Shere especially.

One time I got to the top of this climb to find an ambulance just pulling away, and a couple of cyclists standing about in its aftermath. They told me a middle-aged man had had a heart attack upon reaching the top. I was afterwards unable to find out what had happened to the man, and have since told myself he must have recovered, or else the story would have been newsworthy enough for me to find out more. The road is a steep-enough climb, and an example of a *holloway* to boot, a sunken lane (i.e. hollow way). Over centuries, as muck has been cleared from the road, the banks have built up so that they overlook the road from a height of two or three metres, and are then overgrown with trees, so the climb is both memorably pretty and ominously claustrophobic.

Famously among local cyclists, just before the summit there is a blind left hand bend, after which the gradient gets *really* steep. If you don't change gear before the turn, you'll be walking. I was committed to walking anyway, not having a gear to change into. I remembered the man running his bike up the hill to the Youth Hostel in Dolgellau and got as far as lifting my bike onto my shoulder, but a purposeful stride was as good as I could muster.

Steep descents are even less fun on a fixed wheel. You either pedal as fast as you can while applying the brakes to limit your speed to one that won't cause you physical injury, or you go hard-core, unclip your feet from the pedals entirely, and roll down the hill with your feet nonchalantly propped on the top tube of the bicycle and the pedals going round crazily beneath you. The problem with the latter method is the danger of death or serious injury, since the bike is not as much under control as it could be. The problem with the first method is simply that it's uncomfortable and everyone overtakes you. This danger and indignity dilemma aside, the North Downs came and went, and the sun was still shining when I arrived in Richmond Park at the end of the ride.

The Dunwich Dynamo

I wrote about this event before, at least the 2013 version, in *Virgin*, and it remains one of my favourites, a night-ride from London Fields in Hackney to the Suffolk village of Dunwich, 200km of mostly flat riding with the prevailing wind at your back. I would have used fixed again, but for having to find batteries and lights to cycle through the dark, while my Oak is built for riding at night.

With plenty of long-distance rides under my belt already, I was fitter than perhaps I've ever been for this event, and reached the beach in time to see the sun rise above it. I enjoyed my traditional beans on toast and pot of tea for breakfast – I can't remember how many times I've completed this event and done the same — and then had a little sleep on the beach followed by a swim wearing my cycling shorts. Then I changed into a clean pair of shorts for the ride home.

Riding home is harder, because the prevailing wind is now in your face, and you are riding on your own, without the encouragement of the crowd. My good intentions took me as far as Ipswich, where I decided to bail out and take the train to London. I would be able to spend Sunday afternoon with MGL and Junior.

Sadly, this didn't happen. There was a problem with trains. There is often a problem with trains on a Sunday. For one thing there is less demand than on any other day, and so fewer trains run, and the rail network, or Network Rail as it seems to be known in this era of private enterprise, chooses to do most of its maintenance that day. In addition, on this particular Sunday in July, there is an unusually high demand for passengers taking bicycles on journeys from Suffolk generally, and Ipswich in particular. Rail staff are generally nowadays prepared for the Dunwich Dynamo traffic, but the Sunday maintenance was more of a problem.

The train I wanted had been cancelled. Obviously it wasn't just me that wanted it; there were lots of people, quite a few of them with bikes and the air of not having slept the night before. Not only that but none of the trains were running between Colchester and Chelmsford. There was a replacement bus service. Regrettably the replacement bus service could not accommodate bicycles.

Had I known all this in advance, I wouldn't have bought a ticket, and would have just got on with the job of riding home. Had I known this soon after buying the ticket, I would have asked for a refund and then got on with the job of riding home. As it was, I had by now waited around, eaten a Cornish Pasty and had a cup of tea and I was in passenger mode instead of ride-a-bike mode.

I caught the train to Colchester. So far as that went (i.e. about a third as far as I wanted), all was well. From Colchester I cycled along the A12, lacking the energy to find myself a nicer route. It was miserable. The sky had gone grey, the traffic was continuous, I was tired, etc. Nothing good to say. Arriving at Chelmsford, and locating the station, I then found there were further delays to the train service, and that I would need to wait more than an hour here. I picked up a complaint form while I did that.

I did finally sleep on the train to Liverpool Lime Street and was home in time for a very late afternoon lunch. By this I mean it was a meal that had been prepared with the idea of lunch, and although the time was not really one you would contemplate for the midday meal, it was, at least technically, still afternoon.

Months later, having used the complaint form, I received a rail voucher to cover the full price of my ticket, which was some consolation.

CHAPTER SEVEN

Race Preparations

I decided to enter the Mersey Road Club 24. I'd been toying with the idea for a couple of years, once I'd done LEL and found I seemed to enjoy the ridiculous pursuit of high mileages on a bicycle. Since by this stage of the season I knew I would already have done plenty of long rides, I was probably better prepared for it than I had ever been in my life. Also I have an uncle who has done it every year for a while and I knew he'd be there.

Long rides notwithstanding, I needed to do some preparation. There was no point in just turning up, I wanted a result I could take some pride in, or failing that, a result I didn't need to be ashamed of. In particular, I needed to beat my uncle, who is twenty years older than I am, and further handicaps himself by riding a trike.[34] That was a minimum. As a more ambitious target, I wanted to beat 600 kilometres.

In 1975 the Audax Club Parisien introduced the idea of having to qualify for PBP, with the necessity to complete a 600km randonnée in a time of 40 hours. The only way a British rider could then qualify for PBP without completing a 600km event abroad was to complete more than 375 miles in a 24. Fourteen British riders qualified in this way. Four years later, largely to ensure that British cyclists could qualify for future PBPs, the Windsor-Chester-Windsor 600km was instituted and Audax UK was formed to run it.

I didn't really think 600km was something I was capable of. After all, the Bryan Chapman had taken me 38 hours. But then the Bryan Chapman was much much hillier than the Mersey Wheelers 24 course, and I had not been aiming to complete it in a particularly short time. And sometimes you have to aim, if not for the stars, then at least for low-flying space hardware.

---

[34] For those of you who move in tricycle circles, he is known as trikindave.

A 24 is a simple competition where riders compete to see how far they can ride in a day. The idea is almost as old as the first bicycle, and arguably older if you are particularly argumentative. The first recorded 24 in the UK was in 1882, from London to Bath and back, when it was won by a Mr Snook, who covered a distance of 214 miles.[35]

In terms of preparation, first I needed to take down my lightweight Bianchi road bike from where it had hung in my garage since I finished LEL nearly two years earlier. I'd bought it secondhand for £400 as a stopgap because at the time I only had a mountain bike and a fixie and didn't feel up to riding either over 1400 kilometres. I'd told MGL I would sell it as soon as I got my custom-made road bike, but somehow when that happened I didn't get around to it. Once cleaned of cobwebs and dust, it still looked the part, with shiny Campagnolo[36] components and a cool colour on its lightweight aluminium frame. Unfortunately the shiny Campag wheels, although undeniably still shiny, were otherwise in poor condition. On the front wheel, the rim was dented beyond repair; on the rear, the hub was worn out, loose on the axle and impossible to adjust.

I didn't want to spend (lots of) money on this — the bike was a stopgap after all, and I would be selling it soon, so I asked around at work - a number of my teaching colleagues are keen cyclists. Paul came to the rescue, lending me some fairly lightweight wheels that had been on his race bike until he replaced them with something lighter, faster, and more expensive. I needed to get a new Campag cassette hub and some skinny tyres, but that was all. Then Charlie saw me with Paul's wheels outside the staff common room and said I could do better than that, and promised to lend me her partner's Zipp wheels.

I hesitated. Zipp Cycle Components of Indianapolis, Indiana are famous for high-end road racing carbon-fibre wheels, which sell for upwards of a thousand pounds a pair. I would be terrified of damaging them. And yet I was tempted. Charlie had been until recently a key member of the elite amateur woman's racing team sponsored by the cycle café *Look Mum, No Hands*, of which her partner Sam is joint owner. Sam himself is a very talented cyclist and a top-end bicycle mechanic. Charlie had recently had to stop racing after being diagnosed with breast cancer. After radio- and chemotherapy she was gradually getting back towards cycling fitness, and I had been on a few gentle rides with her. Before she was ill I wouldn't have been

---

[35] British Cycling, of course, is firmly wedded to the measurement of distance in miles. Miles, from the Latin mille, or thousand, the approximate distance of a thousand steps taken by Roman soldiers. Audax embraces the French and their kilometres. Scientists prefer the metric system. It's all too complicated.

[36] The pinnacle of Italian cycle racing componentry.

able to keep up. She was interested in the 24, and asked me how far I expected to ride, what training I was doing, what kind of strategy I had. She insisted I needed the wheels. I put up no further resistance.

Now I needed some tri-bars. Tri-bars (also known as aero-bars, despite the possible confusion with a brand of bubbly chocolate) are prongs protruding from the middle of the handlebars with a cushioned elbow support, and the idea is that you lean forwards on the bike, holding the end of the prongs with a posture very much like that of a downhill skier (only leaning forwards even more). It isn't particularly comfortable, especially for the back, and it is more difficult to control the bicycle riding it this way, but it does make you significantly more aerodynamic.[37] They are called tri-bars because the first people to use them were triathletes in the 1980s, and it was a little while before this technology made its way into the more conservative world of cycle racing by way of American cyclist Greg LeMond. LeMond used them to beat French hero Lauron Fignon by 58 seconds in a time trial stage to win the Tour de France by the narrowest ever margin of 8 seconds. It broke my heart at the time because I was a teenager with an anti-American prejudice and Fignon had glasses like John Lennon and looked so cool.

I had never used tri-bars before. When I last did any competitive cycling, more than twenty years ago, they were still in the future, at least for cyclists in England. Now I was quite childishly excited to tri them out. (Sorry.) I bought the cheapest I could find and mounted them on my Oak bike at first because I still hadn't sorted the wheels out on the Bianchi. Also, I thought it would be safer to practise using these unfamiliar attachments on a bike I was perfectly familiar with.

And it was fun! Very wobbly at low speeds, but once I was moving at a reasonable pace, stable enough. As soon as I ducked down into the low-profile position the tri-bars permitted, there was a very noticeable reduction in the amount of effort I needed to keep the pedals turning at the same rate. For the same effort, I could go perhaps 2 or 3 km/h faster. I knew scientifically that the aerodynamic position would help, but feeling it was quite another matter. I probably looked a bit weird riding to work with them on the handlebars, but on the way home every day I was happy to take a detour through Richmond Park and ride flat out.

---

[37] A common misconception is that a streamlined shape will make you go faster. This is true, but only indirectly so. What the aerodynamics actually achieves is a smaller energy loss when moving through the air at the same speed. A lot of the time, that energy saving is the important thing. For a car, streamlining equates to better fuel consumption. For a golf ball, it means the ball loses its kinetic energy at a lower rate, meaning it can travel further. For me, riding over 24 hours, I was hoping the energy I saved would mean I still had something left to keep racing in the last hours of the event.

I got Paul's wheels fitted to the Bianchi and moved the tri-bars over, and then started doing some proper training sessions, taking in a few laps of Richmond Park once or twice each week. In was the summer term, and with my exam classes now busy taking exams instead of being in lessons, I had a couple of early finishes each week.

On the last day of the school term Charlie brought in the pair of Zipp wheels in their own zip-up wheel bag. The bag with the two wheels inside it weighed about what you would expect one wheel to weigh. And the wheels themselves were things of beauty. Not new, not shop fresh and shiny, but purposeful and beautifully engineered. They were entirely black; black anodised hubs and black spokes flattened in cross-section for better aerodynamics, black carbon rims, and black tyres. The rims were about 10cm deep, and the surface dimpled like a golf ball. As a physics teacher I had recently been explaining to sixth formers just why a golf ball has dimples and how these allow it to move through the air a little quicker.[38]

The following day, I was in the park again, and I swear I could feel these wheels slicing their way through the air. I was convinced I was faster with the tri-bars, and faster still with the Zipp wheels. I knew that at least some of that was due to the placebo effect, but that was okay too.

The placebo effect works because you believe it works. If you investigate the effect and find no justification for that belief, then you undermine your own belief and it will no longer work. Brand name painkillers are generally more effective in tests than chemically identical painkillers, because people *expect* them to work better. Generic painkillers that are mislabelled as brand name products will do equally well. I had no desire to undermine any such unfounded belief so I didn't test how good they were, for example by freewheeling downhill with the Zipps and then with ordinary wheels, doing a proper scientific experiment in the way I teach children they should be done, testing the one variable you are interested in and keeping all other factors constant.

My next concern was the saddle. For many years I have known that after a long ride over flat terrain, my penis will go numb. This is a common problem among male cyclists. Female cyclists often suffer a similar problem to their own parts, and this may be exacerbated if they are inadvertently using a saddle designed for a man. For fairly obvious reasons, men and

---

[38] Something like this: as the air trails around the back of the golf ball, where the surface of the ball dips away, because of a dimple, the pressure is reduced, and the air speeds up. This has the effect of delaying the onset of turbulence. Less turbulence means less air resistance, and therefore the kinetic energy of the ball dissipates more slowly, and the ball travels faster for a longer time. The net result being it goes further.

women require a different shape to their saddles. After LEL, and particularly after the flat Lincolnshire and Cambridgeshire roads right at the end, my penis was numb for a couple of days. Really.

The first time your penis goes numb like this, it is profoundly worrying. I'm sure you will agree. When it gets better all by itself just before you summon the courage to see a doctor, it's a relief, and then you forget about it. After it happens a couple of times, and you mention it, discreetly, to other male cyclists, you find out it's pretty common. Just that nobody talks about it before you ask them. The problem is that the bit of you that sits on the bike seat, technically the perineum, is crammed with blood vessels as well as the perennial nerve which connects to the genitals.

Apparently it's not good for you, squashing your perineum. You can improve things by making sure the saddle doesn't point up at the front, and that your handlebars are not too low. You can get a saddle that is designed to spread the pressure out over other parts of your bum. Properly designed shorts — not just padded, but with the padding carefully designed — are a big help (and frighteningly expensive). You can avoid leaning forwards out of the wind, i.e. riding on the drops or on tri-bars, you can stand up on the pedals frequently or take lots of breaks. Better still, you can ride a recumbent bike or you can give up cycling altogether and do something else.

Riding 1200km through the Scottish Highlands was much less of a problem because with so much climbing, I spent much more time standing on the pedals, giving the blood vessels and nerves a chance to recover. The 24 course was mostly flat, so I wouldn't be standing up much, and I was planning to be crouched down out of the wind as much as possible, and not to be taking much in the way of breaks.

For 24 hours.

To make matters worse, I'd been having increasing numbness problems at the end of long rides this year. Generally I only noticed after I stopped feeling sick a few hours after the event. It was particularly bad after the Bryan Chapman, and it was a couple of days before I had anything like normal sensitivity. I had done everything I could to improve my position on the bike, and I already had the frighteningly expensive cycle shorts. I'd been using a Brooks B17 saddle, a brand and model huge numbers of long-distance cyclists use, and something of a luxury item, but I felt that this was the only area I could make a decent improvement.

I felt the answer was a hole in the saddle.

More and more saddles are being designed with a slot in the centre, parallel with the line of the bicycle, at exactly the place where the rider puts his or her problematic perineum. The

57

rest of the saddle has to do the important job of holding you up, and has to still be strong enough to do that despite having nothing in the middle. This tends to make them expensive. One problem in buying a saddle is that how comfortable it is rather depends on your unique physiology, and the only way to find out for sure if it is comfortable is to use one for a week or so. Unless you are able to borrow exactly the saddle you want to try, the only way to use one for a week is to buy it. The saddle is expensive enough, but it is even more expensive if you can't use it and have to buy another one.

There are a few cycle shops that will lend you a saddle for a week against a deposit. Apparently. I heard about one, and on a Saturday afternoon cycled across London, only to find that it was a service they no longer provided. They did, however, provide some very useful free advice about saddles, one of the show assistants showing me that my Brooks saddle was badly out of adjustment. A Brooks saddle is a big piece of carefully-shaped fat premium leather

stretched between the nose and the heel of a steel frame.[39] There is a screw to keep the leather stretched tight when it sags gradually with age. The screw in mine was not correctly adjusted at all; the saddle was so soft that when I sat on it, the leather sagged until I was resting my most delicate parts against the screw attachments at the nose. I adjusted it immediately. The saddle was imperceptibly more comfortable. After twenty minutes of riding, the difference was more marked, and I could readily appreciate that over several hours it would be still more obvious.

It was a big improvement, and for free, but I decided I would still be safer to choose a saddle with a cut-out. After all, there had been nothing wrong with the saddle two years earlier, for LEL, and I had become numb, and sitting on the saddle more or less non-stop all day and all night was a big ask. I did some internet searching, and then measured the distance between my sit bones (accomplished by sitting for a few minutes on the edge of a Karrimat and then putting a ruler between the dimples my bum made in it). I found a saddle most likely to suit my body shape (tall and painfully thin) and settled on a Specialized Body Fit Romin Pro in the appropriate width.

I'd been told it is a common fallacy that soft equates to comfortable, and there is nothing soft about this saddle. It looks like it has been cleaved in two along its length, the two halves held together with carbon fibre and titanium underneath. I paid more for this saddle than I would for a new Brooks B17 made of thick premium leather, but it is less than half the weight and very sporty-looking, which meant I was further increasing my placebo advantage.

I know you are desperate to find out if this strategy was sucessful, so I'll not withhold information any longer than necessary: at the end of my 24 I had no significant problem with numbness.

---

[39] On more expensive versions, the frame is titanium, making the saddle moderately heavy instead of heavy.

CHAPTER EIGHT

Mersey Roads 24

The event begins and ends in Farndon,[40] Cheshire, a village right on the Welsh border. Apparently Farndon was the location of the first competitive horse race, and nearby Chester Racecourse is the oldest in Britain, with races dating from the sixteenth century.[41]

I drove there. MGL said she could live without the car for the weekend, and I was very grateful. I put my tent in the boot, together with a crate of provisions and a holdall for various items of cycling and non-cycling clothes, put the bike on the bike rack, and carefully stowed the Zipp wheels behind the driver's seat. Off I went.

I enjoyed the drive, listening to an afternoon play on the radio, and then a couple of later Bob Dylan albums. When the satnav showed I was a mile from my destination, I was so much in the zone I was tempted to take a detour to keep driving until the CD finished. The event tomorrow wasn't at the forefront of my mind.

I pulled into the car park of the Farndon recreation ground, and followed the drive around the side of the community building, and I could see my uncle sitting on a deck chair in front of his tent. He'd clearly been there a couple of hours and was reading a book. There were a good half-dozen other tents and campervans in evidence, although clearly the majority of the hundred competitors would be arriving on the day, or they would be staying elsewhere. My uncle had his trike inside the tent, all but filling it, although there was space for his sleeping mat along the side, and if he didn't twist and turn in the night he wouldn't bang his head on any of the wheels. I put up my own tent alongside. Mine was larger than strictly necessary, especially as I did not intend to be sharing it with a bike, let alone a trike.

---

[40] Strictly speaking, it begins in Farndon and ends close by. Exactly where it finishes depends on where a rider is when their allotted 24 hours is up.

[41] Chester Racecourse was supported by the Mayor, Henry Gee, after whom we have the expression gee-gee for horse.

My uncle had already eaten, but he accompanied me to the pub and ate desert while I demolished a large plate of fish and chips and rationed myself to a single pint of beer.

We inspected one another's cycles, like dogs sniffing one another's arses. He worried that Charlie's wheels were too narrow, that they would be such an uncomfortable ride I would suffer for them, losing as much speed through discomfort and subsequent loss of concentration as I gained in aerodynamics. I said they didn't seem to give a particularly harsh ride and told him about the placebo effect. He remained sceptical, but conceded I might have a point.

I looked at his rice pudding delivery system, an adapted water bottle with a long, wide-bore tube system and an air vent so that the rice pudding could be consumed without removing it from the bottle cage. I shared my opinion that I would struggle with the gag reflex if I were to use it. He inspected my rice cakes and approved them, although he warned me he found it difficult to take on board solid food while riding. I was yet to discover this problem.

He was worried about the security of my bike. Although there were a handful of people around, there was no guarantee somebody would always be watching out for the small community of crazy cyclists. His concerns had persuaded me to put the Bianchi in the tent while we went to the pub, just in case. It still had the cheaper wheels on, the Zipp wheels remaining in the locked car, hidden from sight under a blanket. When we were back from the pub and it was time for the long-distance cyclists' early night, I locked the bike between my tent in the car, and tied a length of string to the frame at one end and looped it around my hand at the other. The rope was dark in colour and would-be bicycle thieves were unlikely to see it before a tug on it woke me up to confront them. Exactly how I would confront them, I didn't think about. It seemed ridiculous, but it reassured my uncle, and, I have to admit, me as well.

Of the small community present, my uncle knew everyone, although it was clear he met them only once a year for this occasion. There is generally only one 24 per year in the UK, and the small band of cyclists of this persuasion were thus forced together for this weekend in July every year. They were friendly people too, all of them happy to meet somebody new to the event.

I read for an hour because I had a good book and one of those clip-on reading lights. Completely irrelevant to this book in your hands, I was reading *Packing for Mars* by Mary Roach, an often hilarious account of indignities and logistical problems suffered by astronauts but not widely publicised. Some toilet humour there, too, most of it just floating around. I slept well, probably because the actual reality of the race itself had not penetrated my psyche, although I was also tired from the driving and comfortable in my sleeping bag.

My aim was to sleep for as long as possible into the morning — it was going to be a long day after all — but as long as possible turned out to be only until 8 o'clock. It is difficult to stay asleep in a tent in broad daylight.

My uncle's friend Ian had arrived late in the evening, bringing a stove with him, and so he provided both myself and my uncle with hot beverages to start the day off. Then my uncle and I walked off to his café of choice for pre-24 breakfast, leaving Ian to fry up his own. We walked downhill and out of the village to an old stone bridge over the River Dee where a large signpost Welcomed us to Wales. This bridge was the site of fierce fighting during the English Civil War, I later learned, but a lot of water has passed under it since, and it was utterly quiet.

In the Welsh village of Holt, the favoured breakfast establishment was under new ownership. My uncle was disappointed to hear of the disappearance of the previous owners, but we were nevertheless able to get enormous bowls of superrich muesli and very good coffee. Then we wandered back into England for the 72nd subscription of the Mersey Roads Club 24.

The Mersey Roads Club 24 is called a "subscription" event in that it is funded by donations from cycling clubs and friends and relatives of riders and by riders and ex-riders themselves. The £10 entry fee is only a contribution towards the cost. The event was first held in 1937, filling a gap left by Anfield CC's 24, which had run since 1885 (on that first occasion won by G. P. Mills, who achieved 259 miles on a penny farthing with solid tyres). There were once several 24 hour events running in the UK, but now most years the Mersey Road competition is the only one.

There was some time for fettling first. I had to assemble my bike, carefully taking Charlie's wheels out of their case as if they were museum exhibits, and attaching them to the bike frame. I rode it around the car park to check everything was good, and it was. I was beginning to feel the excitement.

I drove us down to Prees Heath Roundabout to deposit our crates of race supplies. It was for me the first taste of the course. I was driving along what to most people would be an ordinary country road, but for me it was hallowed turf, or hallowed tarmac. As the car followed the gentle undulations of the road I was imagining them on a bicycle, taking in the smoothness of the road, registering the slope of each rise in a way that would never occur to the motorist, or to me driving ordinarily.

Prees Heath Roundabout was an extraordinary place, like an Antarctic research establishment or a military base in a conflict zone, a landscape descended on by people who were milling about purposefully for reasons not altogether clear. An ordinary, if ridiculously over-large, roundabout on an ordinary rural A-road now the centre of intense activity. There were tents and gazebos and parked cars on the neatly mown roadside grass, something itself against the natural order of things, and quite a number of bicycles. But to be more strange, everybody here seemed afflicted with an air of cheerfulness.

I parked on the roundabout itself, two wheels on the grass, in violation of the Highway code, I imagine, but I wasn't the only one. There was a gazebo prominently near the roadside where several people were doing things with camp chairs and boxes, and this was the unsup-ported riders' tent. Unsupported riders were those like my uncle and myself who did not have people with them to have bottles or refreshments or spare clothing or lights or a change of bike ready when necessary, or to shout advice and encouragement along the way. Many riders had a whole crew to support them. Charlie had apologised that she was busy that weekend or she would have come to support me, and I don't doubt that she would. In the event, my uncle and I were early enough we could place our crates in prime locations, in one corner opposite the door, where I would be able to find them whatever my mental state. That done, and a couple of short conversations with people my uncle knew, and we drove back to Farndon.

We picked our numbers up, one large and one small square of nylon bearing the printed number on it, 61 for me, 8 for my uncle. The large one for your back, the small one for your shoulder, the left shoulder because that's the one by the road, where the timekeepers will see it. The squares were fixed to your clothing by a safety pin at each corner so you had to remove your jersey to put it on or else stand very still feeling like a lemon, while a friend/partner/willing other pinned it on for you. This filled ten minutes.

But there were still some hours to kill, and killing them was a difficult thing. I tried lying down, setting an alarm to wake me up in an hour and then giving up on the idea ten minutes later when it was clear I was too wired even to lie down and be still, let alone sleep. I watched others fettle bicycles and then wandered inside the event HQ, now open, where tea and coffee and beer were available (yes to the first) and there was a display of photos from the event's long history, and John Taylor was also there selling his encyclopaedic history of the 24-hour race in Britain. I chatted to him for a while and bought a copy (which I am using now to supply background information).

Eventually the time crept up to 1 o'clock in the afternoon, when the event officially be-gan. My uncle would be eighth off and was ready, riding his bike around the car park. We cycled the short distance to the start line together.

The start was a normally quiet back lane now crowded with parked vehicles and cyclists with and without bicycles, and riders making slow loops up and down with their numbers displayed.

There was a small crowd present to watch George Berwick, the first man off, partly because it signified the beginning and partly because what else was there to do? George won the event back in 1974, and it might be fair to say he is one of the event's characters. Lots of people were taking photos. I did. The chief timekeeper presided at the start, releasing riders exactly on the minute from 1 p.m. onwards. A volunteer held people upright on their bikes for up to a minute before each start, a service not required for my uncle on his trike, or for Jane Moore and Mark Brooking from Willesden CC (number 3) wearing pink jerseys on their tandem trike.

My uncle was off at 1:08, pushing himself gently away from the start.

I stayed for a while, watching. When one of the early riders launched himself into the course, I heard a young boy shouting "Go on, grandad!" I thought that was funny. Whilst the event would inevitably be won by a younger athlete, in terms of age this event was somewhat inclusive.

At number 19 was Simon. He was riding fixed again, but this time a beautiful time trial bike in black carbon fibre and matching Zipp wheels. He represented Chester CC (based near Bristol) but was proudly wearing the cross of St Andrews on his jersey.

After seeing Simon off I drifted back to the tent, short of things to do. I had the best part of half an hour to kill. I decided more calories wouldn't hurt and made myself a bowl of crunchy, high-fat and high-sugar muesli and started chomping it down with another tea from the race headquarters canteen. I started to relax. It was a beautiful warm day and there was a celebratory atmosphere all around.

I was halfway through the cereal when I realised I wouldn't have time to finish it. Nevertheless I needed to get rid of it since I didn't want to return to the smell of the milk soured over a day in the sun. Once I rinsed the plastic bowl I had to put it in the tent lest it blow away.

I arrived at the start just in time to see number 60 riding up the road, and I rolled up to the timekeeper shortly after.

"Cutting it fine," the man said cheerfully as he took hold of my bike by saddle and handlebar. The timekeeper told me I had 20 seconds left.

"Less time to be nervous," I said.

To be honest, waiting beside the timekeeper really is the time to be nervous. Besides the immediate proximity of the ride to come, and the sense that while you are in a place of safety, you are committed now, like a diver standing on the high board, or a parachutist in front of the open hatch, there is also the awkward physical proximity to the stranger who is close enough to smell your fear (and your breath) and who has one hand under your arse.

The Mersey Roads 24 course is made up of three circuits and some connecting road. It starts about half a mile from the race HQ on a side road, turns left to join the B5086 out of the village and left at the next roundabout onto the A534 Wrexham to Crewe road. This section is part of the finishing circuit, and about 23 hours later, each rider will return to this road. The route takes a right at the next roundabout in Broxton and joins the relatively busy A41 going due south through No Man's Heath and Grindley Brook where it joins the Whitchurch Bypass at a round-about 20km into the ride (sorry, I mean about 12 miles). The route follows a number of round-abouts along the A41. Roundabouts are junctions you can negotiate fairly safely at speed if you know what you are doing.

The fourth such roundabout is the one at Prees Heath, and here the Prees Heath Circuit begins.

As I said, the Prees Heath roundabout is huge. I have seen smaller villages. It is very much the nerve centre for the race, with timekeepers stationed here at both sides of it. The unsupported riders' tent is here. On the substantial layby to the south of the roundabout were the camper vans of supporters of some of the competitors. To the north there is a large lorry drivers' café which served free tea and coffee to competitors during the event.

The Prees Heath Circuit takes the A41 south down to Tern Hill, where it ahem... terns right at the roundabout to take the A53, going right at the roundabout in Hodnet onto the A442, and taking this road due south to the roundabout where it meets the B5063 on the outskirts of Wellington, there to turn 180 degrees and head back up north, exactly the way it came south, back to the big roundabout. This circuit is 80km 50 miles in length. In my view, the fact that it uses the same road going south as it does going north, that it does not encompass any mean-ingful area, should disqualify it from counting as a circuit at all, but I would admit that it does successfully give riders 50 miles of safe road to ride fast on.

For the Quina Brook Circuit you go north from Prees Heath as if going back to the race HQ at Farndon but you go left at the next roundabout on a minor road to Tilstock and on to Quina Brook itself, where another left takes riders westwards to Prees Green to join the A49 again to return to Prees Heath. The Quina Brook Circuit is 14 miles long and mostly quiet lanes. A left hand circuit is obviously much safer than a right hand one in countries where we ride on the left.

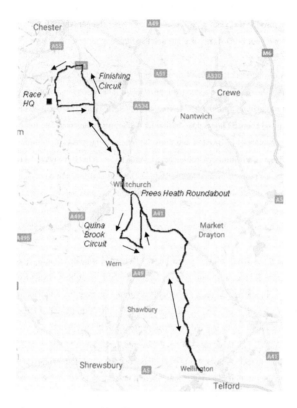

The sequence is something like this: you ride to Prees Heath from the start, do one loop of the Prees Heath Circuit, then from Prees Heath take the Quina Brook Circuit and do some laps of that until it gets dark, when the better-lit main roads of the Prees Heath Circuit are preferred. You do two or three (or more if you're fast) loops of the Prees Heath Circuit until daybreak, and then use the Quina Brook Circuit until, somewhere in the last couple of hours of the event, you are directed northwards to the Finishing Circuit.

The Finishing Circuit starts at the Boxton Roundabout and goes north, making an anti-clockwise loop using the A41 to Hatton Heath, then minor roads through Bruford, Ashford and Farndon. Riders join this circuit and keep circling it until their time runs out.

The timekeeper said the final, "Five, four, three, two, one, go!" and I surged powerfully out onto the course. Or something like that.

Actually nothing like that. I suffer so much from aching joints that I do my best to avoid sudden movements, and also I was well aware that the biggest danger was that I go too fast too soon and burn out early.

But the anxiety was gone and I could enjoy riding.

The first hour was relaxed, although I was surprised to feel so excited about competing. My previous experiences of time trialling, all of them long-ago, were all about pain. A 10 or 25 mile time trial started with pain that very gradually increased in intensity during the event, rising to a crescendo as the end of the course approached. Now I was riding easily, and having to concentrate so I didn't ride too fast. My aim was to average 27 km/h for 22 hours, expecting I might spend one hour in every 12 not actually on the bike. If I kept my speed above 25 km/h on any uphill sections — and there weren't any steep or long gradients so this wouldn't be a problem — then at speeds above 30 km/h I would stop peddling since I would be wasting energy better spent maintaining my speed later in the event. As a general rule, you are better off using most energy at points on the course where you are travelling slowest, because it will affect your average speed more.[42]

It remained a lovely afternoon, and there were people standing at road junctions and laybys cheering me on.

As well as concentrating on the cycle computer on my handlebars, I was keenly looking for direction markers. I was pretty sure of the course, but any mistake would be very costly. The roundabout in the village of Berwick had an A4 laminated sign labelled RTTC 24[43] with an arrow showing me my direction. I followed this, reassured, as I took the third exit. If I could find the signposts easily when I didn't need them, it was a good indication I would be okay when I did. At 10km I turned south on the A49, and the sun in my face prompted me to take my first sip of cola-flavoured caffeinated water.

Prees Heath Roundabout was now alive with activity. There were two volunteers in hi-vis vests as I came on to it and two more where I exited, pointing the way, and to each pair I shouted my number as I'd been told to. Just past Prees Heath, the long layby was lined with

---

[42] As a physics teacher a trick question I like to ask is this: if you are on a 60 mile journey, and drive the first 30 miles in an hour, how fast do you have to drive the rest of the way to average 60 mph?

[43] RTTC stands for the Road Time Trials Council and was the body overseeing the organisation of time trials in the UK until 2002, when it was superseded by Cycling Time Trials. Whoever made the laminated signs either didn't know about the new name or didn't care for it.

spectators sitting in deck chairs or standing, all of them shouting encouragement — perhaps cynically confident that my progress was no threat at all to the riders they were supporting, but nonetheless generous. There was an overwhelming sense of goodwill.

Somewhere along this stretch I caught my first rider. As I approached him slowly, the difference in our relative speeds not overly great, I made sure the animal instinct to kill did not cause me to go faster than myself-imposed limits. I thought calling out encouragement might seem arrogant, because for all I knew I might be unable to hold this pace and he might go on to overtake me repeatedly during the night and all the following morning, so instead, I wished him "Good Day!" in the English manner.

The long stretch south of Prees Heath was the busiest in terms of traffic, and to me the least enjoyable. There was a constant flow of cars and lorries in either direction. On a positive note, on this section there were riders coming the other way on the far side of the dual carriage-way, those on the return half of the Prees Heath Circuit. I tried to keep my eyes out for my uncle, or Simon, or anyone I recognised, but without success.

I passed other riders. Riders passed me. The ones I passed were older than me, some of them had possibly been competing before I was born. Those who passed me did so at speed, wearing club colours, aerodynamic helmets, and a sense of purpose. Few of them said anything as they passed, lest it interfere with their focus.

I tried to estimate when I would first see my uncle. I'm good at mental calculations while I'm cycling. By this I don't mean I can accomplish feats of arithmetic despite the distraction of movement and effort, but that I can find a series of simple calculations thoroughly diverting for considerable periods of time. The calculations went like this: If I were able to achieve 600km in 24 hours, as I was aiming to do, and my uncle 300 miles, i.e. 480km, as he had done in the last few years, then the ratio of our speeds would be, now let me think, yeah, 4/5, meaning about every five minutes I'd be gaining a minute on him (or every five kilometres I'd catch up by one). Here I was making the giant assumption both he and I would keep a constant speed throughout the event, or else that we would tire at exactly the same rate. He had started $61 - 8 = 53$ minutes ahead of me, which meant I should expect to see him after 212 minutes, or three and a half hours.

An added complication, I realised after I'd reached the roundabout at the southern end of the Prees Heath Circuit, was the possibility I would catch him when I was on my first circuit of the Quina Brook loop and he on his second. I tried to get my head around the numbers, reckoning that, at his speed of $300/24 = 12.5$mph, the Quina Brook Circuit represented $14/12.5$

= 1.2, that is, just over an hour. So the answer was no, since I'd started less than one hour behind him.

Paradoxically, if my sole intention was to catch him as fast as possible, the best plan would have been to start at a speed somewhat less than my uncle's so I could arrive at the start of the Quina Brook Circuit just as he was starting his second lap, and at that point increase my speed to whatever maximum I might expect to maintain for the remaining 21 hours of the event.

By the time I had come to a conclusion, I had returned to Prees Heath, shouted "61" at the men and women in hi-vis and been directed down Tilstock Lane into the Quina Brook Circuit, and the small winding roads made the calculation is more difficult. Because of the delay and the fact that probably most of my brain activity had shut down due to some evolved survival mechanism to keep my pedalling muscles energised, I was only just through with the final check on my calculations when I did indeed pass my uncle crouched over his antique trike. It was much earlier than I had expected, I thought, until I checked the clock and found it just about right.

Other calculations were about my own progress. I had covered just over 100km in three hours and 40 minutes. If I could do this five more times I would indeed achieve 600km, allowing that I could have 20 minutes off every four hours. I hadn't stopped once yet, but I would at the completion of my first Quina Brook lap since I needed more water. I had half my bottles filled with cola-flavoured water doped with caffeine, and half of them pure H_2O, and I thought I was drinking almost as much water as I was sweating out. As the day drew on and it became cooler I would do better on that score, so I wasn't worried about getting overly dehydrated. Food was another matter. I had been proud of my economical and nourishing rice cakes, but so far I had only managed to eat one of them. They took too long to chew and to swallow, and in the meantime I needed my mouth for breathing. It was also easy to feel nauseous when eating. Instead of rice cakes, I'd had an energy gel which was disgusting but easy for the body to process, and a Snickers bar which was more difficult, but still easier than the rice cake.

The Quina Brook Circuit was a little uncomfortable with the high-pressure narrow-tyred Zipp wheels, and I needed to pay good attention to the road to avoid potholes that might threaten a puncture or worse. Worse being personal injury, or a broken wheel and having to apologise to Charlie. But this circuit was made up of lovely country lanes with pretty thatched houses and was almost completely devoid of traffic, and it was easy to enjoy, even mid-race.

The phenomenon that is trikindave. Picture by David Goodfellow

At the roundabout I stopped for my first pit stop, taking the two bottles out of their cages on the bike and having them in my left hand as I came to a halt and dismounted. I might have considered running the 20 steps to the unsupported riders' tent if my legs hadn't made a sudden and unexpected objection. I decided not to labour the point and allowed them to walk me there. I tossed the empty bottles into the space just behind my provisions crate and picked up one of four bright yellow bonk bags, and, slinging this over my shoulder, got back on the bike and made my way around the rest of the roundabout, shouting "61" at the right place, and starting my second circuit of Quina Brook.

A bonk bag, or musette, to give it its official name, is a small cotton bag about the size of a folded newspaper with an opening at the top and a shoulder strap. Mine cost me £4 in total by mail order and I had loaded them each with two bottles (one water, one cola flavour) two rice cakes, a granola bar, and a Snickers. Actually, two of the bags had a banana instead of the Snickers. A balanced diet. Now, while moving, I transferred the bottles to the bottle cages on my bike and the solid "food" to my jersey pockets, this whole exercise probably saving me up to 45 seconds and thus, potentially, 400m. For four bonk bags, that would amount to almost a mile. In a professional race, riders would throw the empty bonk bag to the side of the road, where it would be picked up and treasured by an eager follower of the sport. I figured if I threw mine down, aside from the £1 cost, I would be contributing to the litter problem, so I folded the bag up and stuffed it into my already overstuffed pockets.

A little under an hour later, after my second Quina Brook Circuit, I took a detour off the route to the transport café that did indeed give me a free cup of tea. That I had to travel 200m off the course, and then 200m afterwards to get back onto it, more than made up for the bonk bag manoeuvre. But a good cup of tea will sort most things out, and I figured I had made good enough time to allow such decadence. I managed to eat a whole rice cake and a granola bar with it as well, which was a bonus.

I did a third and possibly fourth lap of Quina Brook in the late afternoon and early evening before I stopped at the tent. It was a lot cooler now, and I put on my leggings and arm-warmers and swapped the bottle I'd emptied for a full one. A woman volunteer asked me if I had a reflective jacket and I answered her that I had, putting my yellow Gore-Tex jacket into my pocket. She didn't seem impressed by this and told me I should have "proper reflective strips".

I thought I would still be on the Quina Brook Circuit after this, but as I came to the northern part of the Prees Heath roundabout, the timekeepers pointed me around further onto the Prees Heath Circuit. I had heard something about an accident somewhere near Quina Brook, a rider suffering broken forks, which sounded bad to me, and I put two and two together and decided we were being moved off that circuit while a medical emergency was sorted out. I found out later nobody was seriously hurt (although without a spare bike, broken forks must be the end of a rider's event) and that the organisers always switch to the Prees Heath Circuit before it gets dark rather than after.

A while later I had to stop for my first pee stop. My uncle had told me a pee stop takes two minutes all told, including the slowing down and stopping, and the starting off from stationery afterwards. That's if you get off your bike; it takes about one minute if you don't. The difference, at my kind of speed, is about a quarter of a mile. I had decided independently that on a quiet enough stretch of road there was no need to dismount in search of privacy, just pull up off the road and point away from the traffic.[44] I noted that my cycle computer, which stopped its timer automatically when I stopped moving, clocked my pit stop as a minute almost exactly. If you include the slowing down and the speeding up, my stop was longer than my uncle's, but I may have had more liquid to dispense with.

---

[44] It might be noted this pointing business is probably not an option for a woman. Allowing four stops for a dehydrated competitive cyclist over 24 hours, that's at least a mile penalty.

It grew dark, and as it did, it started raining. I had to slow down while I pulled my GoreTex jacket out of the rear pocket and put it on. Cycling in the rain is horrible, but it's only horrible until every part of you that can get wet has got wet. After that, it's merely unpleasant.

I passed my uncle again. By now he was also in yellow, and his trike was bejewelled with lights, a splendid sight in the dark. In the darkness I was to make the observation that the slower riders, i.e. those that I passed, were generally illuminated like Christmas trees, with lights often on helmets, handlebars, forks, seat stays and under the saddle, whereas those riders who over-took me tended to carry the legal minimum, a single bright, but not spectacular, front light, a single rear.

The rain was unrelenting. I felt my socks gradually fill with water until I could feel the water squirting out through the drain holes in the bottom of my shoes, one squish each time I pushed down on a pedal. I felt the damp begin to creep into my arms as the Gore-Tex was tested beyond the limit of its waterproofing. At some point in the middle of the night I decided to stop at the café again. Despite the lower temperature, I was still not managing to eat solid food while on the bike, and I worried about my blood sugar level failing. I dripped into the huge, mostly empty café, leaving my bike unlocked just outside the door where it was out of the rain.

"Have you packed?" The guy who served me had a tone that seemed to offer condolences.

"No. I just fancy a break."

This time I had beans on toast as well as tea. I felt a little guilty for taking the time off, as if those of us racing had a duty to perform. But I remember one of my uncle's stories about supporting a friend who was riding a 24 but declared he'd had enough and was packing. They took him into the back of the campervan and fed him soup and a sandwich while letting him believe he *had* packed, and then, when he was least suspecting it, they put him back on his bike and pushed him off into the darkness.

The pot of tea and a plate of baked beans made me feel a whole lot better, although I did feel guilty, as I have said, feeling that athletes should not be sitting down to a meal in the middle of an event. As I made my way out of the door I met a miserable looking motorcyclist. I smiled him a smile I hoped conveyed a little of a sense of commiseration. It was a horrible night to be out, all the more so if you were volunteering rather than competing.

I did the Prees Heath Circuit again, and indeed again. At the roundabout I took care to shout my number as clearly as possible, although, as it turned out, not as clearly as necessary. I could hear the timekeepers asking for my number after I had gone past, after I had shouted my "61", and I shouted again, despite knowing that my shout would be lost in the wind and the rain. But

I wasn't going to go around the roundabout a second time to make sure of passing on the information.

Eventually the weather got better. The rain got less. It is the sort of thing you don't notice for a while, and then you do, and you think, "At least it's not raining quite as hard as it used to be."

And then there was a hint of daylight creeping into the darkness. With the aid of this light I noticed a large tent beside the roundabout at the southernmost end of the Prees Heath Circuit, a frame tent very much like the one my family spent holidays in when I was a child. Inside it were a couple of tables with all the apparatus you might associate with the production of hot beverages. There were also a few deck chairs, and in one of them sat my uncle. A hitherto unsuspected refreshment point. Had I been aware of this, I am sure I would have saved a good five minutes by not visiting the transport café, and would have achieved at least one extra mile. For here was that delight of delights, hot tea, and at a distance of less than three metres from the course. If you are not aware of the intense joy that can be provided by a steaming mug of tea and a chair in a tent in the middle of a wet night then I feel sorry for you because you have not yet lived.

"How are you doing?" My uncle asked me. "You look like you're going well."

And I was. I had been continuing with my calculations all the while as I made my way through the soggy night, noting how far I had travelled every time I passed under the bright streetlamps around Prees Heath, when could see the numbers on my cycle computer. I was very comfortably on course to achieve 600km, and had for a while been wondering if 400 miles (aka 640km) was possible. At this time it seemed unlikely, but not implausible.

"And what about you?"

Something of a sigh. "I started too quickly, and I'm paying for it."

He didn't look too miserable, though, and I got the impression he was more happy about my good fortune than he was upset about his own lack of it.

The two guys in the tent dishing out the tea — lovely people, but I can't remember anything much about them — were talking about Steve Abraham, who had apparently spent several hours asleep in the corner of the tent earlier on. My uncle had obviously been making calculations himself during the night, and reckoned that Steve would have achieved a greater mileage towards his annual goal if he had ignored the 24 altogether and maintained his usual routine, but the feeling in the room (I mean tent) was that, the One Year Record notwithstanding, he didn't want to miss a year from the 24.

73

I was ready to leave but then Simon arrived, which was a good excuse for a second mug of tea. Simon was also disappointed in his progress. "I just seem to be going slow. I don't know why." He was on course for less than 500km when his ambition had been 600km like mine. He did confess that his brakes seemed to have been on slightly the whole time so far.

"That could be something to do with it, "

I was very reluctant to leave the warm camaraderie of the tent, but it was necessary.

By the time I reached the Prees Heath roundabout, it was daylight enough not to need lights on, which was just as well, considering that the batteries had almost gone. I stopped at the tent and dropped off the lights, making my bike several hundred grams lighter and perhaps a touch more aerodynamic. I left the hi-vis GoreTex behind too and swapped a half-empty water bottle for a full one, and picked up a couple more energy sachets, which probably meant a zero change on the weight factor. I didn't need to reload with delicious rice cakes because I hadn't managed to eat any during the night, but now, with the optimism that comes with daylight, I wasn't worrying about it. There were only eight hours left, and I still had strength; I didn't think I was going to collapse through lack of energy.

I did another 50 mile circuit of the Prees Heath loop and at the end of it the marshals marshalled me back onto the Quina Brook Circuit. Over the course of the morning I must have made a few more laps there. I managed to eat several more granola and Snickers bars and, with some effort, two rice cakes. The thing about granola and Snickers is that, being relatively dry, you can take a mouthful and push the rest back into your pocket, whereas the rice cakes crumbled. Plus granolas and Snickers give you more of a sugar buzz than cheesy rice does.

I passed Steve Abraham, somewhat to my surprise. Since, in each of the previous two years, he'd achieved nearly 450 miles, I thought he would be moving considerably faster than me, and he should have been, probably, if he were truly on course to beat Tommy Goodwin's record. I would pass him again a couple more times before the finish.

I'd been cold towards the end of the night, and it took me awhile to warm up. Now I was riding in three-quarter length cycling tights and a long sleeve cycle jersey, all in black with the sun warming me,[45] and despite a quiet burning sensation in my legs I was very comfortable. Mental calculations both entertained me, and gave me reassurance I remained on schedule for my 600km. As the morning wore on, however, the goal of 400 miles looked further and further

---

[45] The colour black makes an excellent absorber of thermal radiation, as I am required to teach schoolchildren.

away, and this also came as a reassurance: If 400 miles was unlikely, there was no reason to kill myself trying to achieve it.

When the marshals at the Prees Heath roundabout sent me north towards the finishing circuit, it came as a surprise. The final stage of the event already!

The change of road, and the good surface on the A49 gave me the encouragement to up my effort, at least for a few minutes. When I reached the finishing circuit, there were more people cheering at the side of the road. They were mostly supporters of one or another of the riders rather than what you might call genuine spectators, but they *were* people, and they were cheering. Some of the people were official timekeepers — I think there were four of them around the circuit — and they were cheering too. One of them even had a hand bell, the kind we had in primary school to call is in from break, to offer more audible encouragement.

The finishing circuit had a rougher surface than I had been enjoying previously, and it was more rolling, although these observations may have more to do with my state of tiredness than with the local geography. When I passed 600km I felt the merest shrug of happiness at reaching a goal I had, only the previous day, considered possibly over-ambitious, and, having achieved it, my motivation took a dip. I became more and more aware of the pain in my legs. My arms ached from holding my position on the tri-bars, and it was increasingly difficult for me to hold an aerodynamic position.

It was also more difficult to focus, and I found myself on occasions freewheeling, or soft-pedalling without meaning to. I tried to set myself a new targets; 380 miles came easily, then 610km, then 620km. I tried to focus on 390 miles, but these numbers seemed arbitrary, hugely more arbitrary than nice round numbers like 600 or 400. Clearly I didn't want to achieve 390 miles enough, because I didn't quite get there and, cutting out a few episodes of soft peddling would have made the difference.

To make the closing stages more entertaining, I now noticed my handlebars had worked themselves loose, and were gradually rotating. My arms rolled forwards with them. Having to readjust the handlebars every few minutes wasn't the hardest chore, since the tri-bars made a convenient lever to haul them back into position, but it didn't help me concentrate, and neither

The author on the finishing circuit. Picture by David Goodfellow.

did my worry about whether they would work themselves loose enough to be dangerous. I considered stopping to tighten the relevant Allen bolt, and decided against it. This proved to be the correct decision, since subsequent investigation at home showed the bolt had been stripped of its thread and tightening it was no longer possible.

Cycling past the event headquarters was exciting, because there was a true crowd there, and huge encouragement was shouted and clapped every time I went past. The boost this gave me lasted at least a couple of more miles, especially as straight afterwards I could turn onto the relatively fast A534. But the boost would be over before I made the next turn and I bumbled and coasted my way back around the finishing circuit.

Eventually the stopwatch on my Garmin unit registered 24:00 and my watch showed 14:01, and the next timekeeper I came to didn't need to signal me to stop, I was freewheeling to a halt anyway, eyeing up the oh-so-comfortable-looking grass verge next to a parked caravan.

I climbed painfully off of my bike and leant it up against the stone wall of a church. I didn't know it at the time, I didn't know very much about anything, but I was just outside St Mary's Church in the village of Bruera. My timekeeper, a very sympathetic middle-aged woman, urged me to sit down and recuperate for a few minutes. I had no intention of doing anything else, but appreciated her kindness.

She was established here in this corner of an English village with car and caravan, a camp chair and table. She had two large German shepherds sitting in the shade.

Some minutes later,[46] Matthew Scholes finished at the same place, and joined me on the grass bank. He looked a lot better than I felt.

"You all right?"

"I'm enjoying sitting here."

We exchanged what distances we thought we had achieved. We were both very happy with our result. He had not only done a personal best, and beaten his three teammates, but broken his club's record. Matthew rides for South Western Road Club, a club based close enough to where I live for me to consider it for myself. He'd done sixty miles more than I had, and in fact he came tenth overall.

There was no phone reception where we were sitting. Matthew walked around the corner to phone his wife, who was going to give him a lift back to the race HQ. I wanted to phone MGL, partly because she worries about me sometimes and mostly because I wanted to share how I'd done. I could see Matthew had got sufficient reception just a few metres away, but my desire to stay sitting down was stronger.

"Do you want a lift?" He offered when he'd finished the phone call.

"Well . . ."

The race HQ was four miles away. You might say that if you've just cycled the best part of 400 miles, then another four isn't anything to get upset about, but once you've stopped, and got off the bike, and enjoyed not cycling for a few minutes, it is significantly more of a deal. Matthew said it wasn't a problem. When he added that I looked like I could do with it, I wasn't insulted.

---

[46] 23 minutes after me, to be exact.

We had to wait for his wife to get here, but waiting really wasn't an issue. Sitting in the sunshine and not cycling was exactly what I wanted to do for a while.

The race was coming to an end. Mrs Timekeeper was getting ready to leave once she heard on her CB radio that all the riders had finished. She opened the tailgate of her car and called her dogs to get in and they jumped into the back in perfect synchronicity, as one, as if they had spent years choreographing it. I commented on this.

"They're marvellous, aren't they?" she said. "They were my husband's, he trained them."

Her husband had died in the last year, and this was the first Mersey Roads 24 since.

"I was dreading it," she said, "but I couldn't not come. And it's been really nice."

I found this very touching. It reminded me of the sense of community this annual event inspired. I could see why my uncle came year after year.

Matthew's wife arrived and she and her husband made short work of putting two bikes on the bike rack, and then I was once again in the back seat of somebody's car thinking it would be rude to fall asleep there.

Back in Farndon, I left my bike between the car and the tent and found myself some tea. I called MGL and she had to listen to me recounting my experiences in a semi-coherent way. I removed the Zipp wheels from the bike and put them carefully in their bag, locking that in the car. I put the other wheels on my bike and propped the bike up against the car. Then I found the civilian clothes I had laid out ready the previous day. The shower was a painful experience due to my having to reach every part of a body much in need of washing but in no condition for the necessary stretching and contortions. But this detail aside, I felt so much better for being clean.

As I sealed my sweaty cycling gear into an airtight bag, I heard people talking about a provisional finish list. Despite knowing how far I had cycled, at least to the nearest mile, I was still eager to see this figure written down. Therefore I went into the bar, and figured that the tight crowd of people in one corner was the place to be.

It was. Cyclists and cyclist-supporters were all struggling to get a view of a sheet of paper held by a man in the dayglo yellow of authority. The paper seemed to be a spreadsheet written and calculated manually, and each rider on the start sheet had their time written in the column on the right. When I finally got to see it, my distance was recorded as 289 point something miles.

"But that's not right!" I protested.

"What should it be?"

"A hundred miles more than that."

"You'll have to talk to the chief timekeeper then."

To find the chief timekeeper I had to find a small windowless room in the middle of the building, marked "No Entry", a room I imagined would be easy to defend against a rioting mob. There were two men in there, both, as MGL would say, of a certain age, both still wearing their yellow vests. I never did find out which of them was the chief timekeeper.

By this time I had worked out what had happened. 100 miles was exactly two times the length of the Prees Heath Circuit, so clearly on two occasions at the Prees Heath roundabout I had failed to make my number clear to the timekeepers there. All I needed to do was to explain this.

"You should have shouted your number out."

"I did. Just not loud enough."

"You should have had your number pinned to your jersey."

"I was wearing my GoreTex over my jersey."

"Why didn't you pin your number to your jacket?"

"If I put holes in it, it wouldn't be so waterproof."

One of them said that was the price you had to pay. The other said, "You could have left the jacket off and taken the weather like a man." They were clearly a double act.

"But then I would have been too cold to race. I probably could only have ridden 280 miles then."

"Then we wouldn't have a problem."

You don't stay up all night watching cyclists ride around without having a sense of humour to keep yourself amused. Joking aside, they looked at the split times for number 61 and saw that either I'd found somewhere to have a six hour kip in the middle of the night, and then turned up again at exactly the right time and place to maintain the average speed I'd been setting, or I had indeed gone around the Prees Heath Circuit twice without being recorded. My distance would be amended. Since I was in no danger of worrying the prize list, it didn't make for a controversial decision in any case.

At that point I headed back to the bar, passing a sleeping Steve Abraham on a chair in the corridor outside, and treated myself to a pint of beer.

At the prizegiving ceremony I learnt that the event had been won by Michael Broadwith who achieved the quite ridiculous distance of 537.35 miles, the second greatest ever achieved. Only a handful of riders have ever beaten 500 miles, and to do so in such poor weather conditions was remarkable. All the more so because Michael was riding his first ever 24. Although he had passed me probably a dozen times during the day, I didn't recognise him as he collected his trophy, but that was partly because he had been wearing a skinsuit and aero helmet on the bike, and he'd generally come past me so fast he was gone before I registered he was there.

There were no prizes for third fastest teacher or for the second fastest tricycle, so neither myself nor my uncle collected silverware. But I did come 33rd out of about 100 competitors, and I was pretty happy with that.

I went to the pub with Uncle and Ian, walking slowly across the recreation ground and up the High Street to get there. My legs were not in a great deal of pain, but they certainly gave me interesting sensations. I was in good shape, I decided. I could walk. My bum was no more than slightly sore, and I had no loss of sensation in my penis, which I think represented £100 well spent. At the pub, I surprised myself by not having enough appetite for anything more than a normal meal. I decided a second pint in the afternoon was enough as well. All in all, a very model of moderation.

It was about 8p.m. when we got back to the event HQ. The building was locked up, and only those people camping onsite were still around. The sun was still in the sky, but it was bedtime nevertheless.

Just as I was lying down in my sleeping bag my phone rang. It was Charlie, keen to know how I'd got on. That she was genuinely impressed and happy for me was quite touching when both she and her partner were cyclists who actually won events rather than simply took part in them.

I woke up about eight o'clock in the morning, which surprised me. I had the idea I might have slept until noon or something like that. But I was awake, and didn't have any desire to lie in. I could hear my uncle snoring in the next tent.

I got up and dressed, and when I came out into the grey morning I saw Ian was up, setting his kettle on the camping stove. He offered me tea. I put the tent down, doing it quietly as I didn't think it fair to wake my uncle up, although I seemed to remember Grandma saying that after he'd cycled home overnight from Chelmsford to Bristol,[47] something he did regularly as a young man, he could not be woken.

---

[47] A distance of 270km. He would set off at 10pm, and ride through the night, arriving for breakfast. When I was a young man I was wealthy enough to use trains.

I had everything packed away, and my bike secured to the back of the car by the time Ian had the tea ready. We chatted in quiet voices, the car park silent and the recreation ground around us empty bar a woman in the distance walking her dog. Apparently I had said something like "if I do this again" the previous evening, and he reminded me of that. I had always thought this would be the one and only time I did a 24, but, as Ian was reminding me, it didn't appear to be the case. By riding 389 miles I had left myself unfinished business. One day I will have to do 400.

I hoped that my uncle would wake in time for me to say goodbye, but I wasn't going to hang around for a couple of hours just to give him that chance. Not when there are perfectly good electronic communication systems. I drove home happily listening to very loud music, and stopping just once for double espresso.

CHAPTER NINE

Majorca

We went to Majorca for ten days. MGL booked a flight about as early as she felt it would be safe for me to travel after the 24. I'm not entirely sure what post-endurance sport symptoms might make flying difficult but went along with her arrangements, and we flew the day after I'd returned home.

Majorca is a remarkably cheap place to fly to for a short holiday, because there is a huge market for holiday makers there. The majority of British holidaymakers seem to have no interest in being somewhere overseas except for the sunshine, cheap food and alcohol, and proximity to the sea, and the tourist industry caters for this need. From a cheap hotel built around a small swimming pool, however, it is only necessary to travel the shortest of distances, and perhaps to catch a bus, to be somewhere else entirely.

And Majorca is an amazing place to ride a bike. It has plenty of roads, and little traffic, it has the climate, in particular the lack of rain, and it has excellent climbs and some spectacular scenery. As a result it is increasingly popular with professional cycling teams for training camps and with amateur cyclists for cycling holidays. It is possible to hire an excellent road (or mountain) bike for a reasonable rate, one that makes transporting your own bike an unnecessary hassle.

We stayed in the town of S'Illot on the east coast of the island. The town's principle industry is, of course, tourism, but there is a working boatyard as well, and some fishing. The coach journey that came free with the flights and the hotel took an age to get there via half a dozen other hotels, but we were half asleep while it did that. The hotel was clean and functional, and there was even intermittent Wi-Fi available in the bar so Junior was able to keep up with social media. I had no real interest in cycling for a couple of days after arriving, and was content to enjoy the sunshine and the cheap food and alcohol, as well as swimming in the sea, all of which felt good while my legs recovered. We did, however, visit the more interesting town of Porto Cristo (the name dates back to the Christian invasion of Mallorca in 1260 AD, and there is a legend of a fishing boat found washed up on the beach containing a crucifix).

I rented a bike for the final week and covered over 400km on it. I'd intended to try out something flash in carbon fibre but instead elected for a perfectly adequate lightweight aluminium frame bike which was much newer than what I'd just done the Mersey Roads 24 on, and had a cycle computer attached already. One thing the shop was unable to provide was a bidon or two, and I had forgotten to bring mine, but the proprietor assured me that any standard mineral water bottle would fit into the bottle cages. This turned out to be a practical, although by no means stylish, solution, so it was probably for the best that I rented a relatively budget machine. I rode it every day, if only for an hour before MGL and Junior were ready for their breakfast, but a couple of times I went on longer excursions.

The first of these was to the south of the island, a long flat ride through rural farmland, punctuated with a stop in the small town of Santanyi for a *bocadillo* (sandwich) and for a swim at the *Platja es Caragol* or beach of the snail, and returning via the wonderfully-named towns of Felantix and Manacor.

On finishing this ride, and carrying the bike up the single flight of concrete stairs to our apartment, the sole of my right shoe came away from the rest of it. The shoe made a comical flapping sound as I walked in. This might have represented something of a problem since the nearest bike shop I knew of was in Manacor, 15km away, and I wasn't convinced they would have SPD cycling shoes my size. MGL, however, suggested it might be possible to buy some superglue and make a temporary fix, and indeed this turned out to be the case.

The other ride was to see the amazing Cap Formentor, the northernmost point of the island. I went by way of the medieval town of Artà, whose Santuari de Sant Salvador and ancient fortifications atop the town's hill dominates the landscape. I didn't visit these attractions, but stopped in a cycle shop in an attempt to find new shoes. I had a late second breakfast in a café, and read in a local newspaper about Chris Froome's winning of the Tour de France, and then went on through Alcúdia, a large resort town we'd visited many years earlier, then to Port de Pollença, the most northerly town in the island, and the only one in which an Agatha Christie story is set. I had lunch here outside the supermarket where I bought it, made sure my temporary mineral water bottle bidons were full, and set off up the forbidding-looking road into the *Serra de Tramuntana*, the mountainous spine of the island that runs all along the northwest coast. From Port de Pollença the road climbs and twists and zig zags for 20km out along the peninsula, giving jawdropping views of the sea, first on one side and then on the other, finally snaking up to the lighthouse at the end, which stands atop 200m cliffs over the sea. For the last kilometre I needed to thread my way past the queue of traffic waiting to get into the car park. There is a café there, and places to sit, and balconies to lean over to admire the views and take photographs. There are also goats to eat any foodstuffs tourists drop or otherwise leave behind.

When I stopped to buy some more water in Port de Pollença I took this picture, which gives you an insight into the resourcefulness of goats, and shows why you should be careful where you park your car.

Note how the goats' cloven hooves have made a pleasing dappled effect of small dents all over the bonnet and roof of the car.

I went back more or less the same way, stopping several times to buy liquids, since it was fiercely hot by this time, and I was pleased to have clocked up 180km all told. According to Google Maps, there was 2140m of climbing, so I'd have racked up a couple of AAA points if I'd done it as an Audax permanent.

CHAPTER TEN

To Paris

A few days after I came back from Majorca I bought a new pair of cycling shoes. The fact that I had now taken up cycle racing had obviously made a big impression on me, for instead of replacing like with like, I bought a pair of ultra-lightweight racing shoes instead of a pair I could walk in without fear of injury. After all, I was going to do my second race, the Catford Hill Climb, later in the season.

I spent a good half hour trying on pairs of shoes, trying two different sizes, worried that I might get a size that was slightly too small for me. Then I bought a pair of shoes slightly too small for me. Only later did I find that the ultra-lightweight design included a nice smooth surface on the underside so that if you didn't hit the cleat on the pedal exactly, your foot slipped off it entirely, with the usual result that I cracked my ankle against something hard and metallic or that I didn't hit my ankle on anything but almost fell off the bike, saving myself by catching the nose of the saddle with my genitals. I think the idea behind this is to motivate the would-be racing cyclist to learn how to get their foot in the cleat first time, thus avoiding losing precious seconds in race situations.

After PBP and the Catford Hill Climb, these shoes have been moved to the attic.

Having done a 1200km audax through northern Scotland the year before, sleeping in a bivvy bag and prepared to carry any food I needed, I had a very good idea of what I needed to take with me for PBP. Nevertheless, I gave the matter renewed consideration, especially in the light of a long article published for this very purpose.

Audax UK is a self-help organisation for cyclists who wish to cycle long-distance. Most of the long-distance rides I do are organised by them. Members receive, for the £19 annual subscription, a free quarterly magazine, *Arrivée*, full of colour photographs of people riding bicycles and articles of variable quality. Marcus JB, whom I'd met on the aforementioned Scottish audax had written a comprehensive and uniquely personal list of items a cyclist might take on PBP, which was published in the spring edition of *Arrivée*, and was by far the most entertaining piece in that edition. It was undoubtedly useful, especially for people who had not done a multistage long-distance ride before, although I found Marcus's persuasive writing made me take one or two items I had no need of and leave behind some that I did. Marcus also intended abstaining from coffee for several months before the event, so his body was not acclimatised to caffeine and he could more usefully drink the stuff to keep himself awake. I felt that was dedication over and above the call of what was necessary. Later, I would come to realise how sensible his advice might have been.

The only way to get to Paris for the start of PBP is to cycle there. Of course that is not strictly true, but to do anything else seemed to me (at this particular time in my life) to be somehow betraying the purity of the endeavour. Something like that.

Actually cycling to the start makes a lot of sense, especially when you start thinking about the alternatives. Alternative one is to travel to the start by car. Obviously this adds an expense, because you have to pay for the car to go across on the ferry, and you have to pay to park the car for five days. And you have to ask if you will be fit enough to drive the car back when physically exhausted and sleep-deprived. If you only have one car, you need to persuade your wife/husband/significant other that they don't need it for the week. I did consider persuading MGL that it would make a nice family break for her and Junior to make the trip with me, but only very briefly. Alternative two is to take your bike with you by train. Or more precisely to take your bike with you by train, ferry, and another train, after which there is still the 46km ride from Gare du Nord station in Paris to the start at St Quentin-en-Yvelines. And taking a bicycle by train is not always straightforward, either in England or in France.

Both alternatives required considerably more hassle and more expense, if less in the way of physical effort or time. And surely cycling to Paris would be an excellent warm up for the event itself.

It would have been simple to have hitched up with some other people who were doing the same thing. These other people were making arrangements on forums like yacf,[48] and on

---

[48] Yet Another Cycling Forum. Really. The successor to Cycling Forum and Another Cycling Forum, this is currently the go-to forum for information on this kind of cycling, although obviously at some point omgnacf will supersede it.

Facebook,[49] but as I may have mentioned before, I am not terribly good at organisation.

I'm pretty good with maps though. Possibly over-confident in my ability with them, and perhaps over-reliant on the information they present. Nevertheless I set to working out a route to get me to the start.

I booked the ferry, the 22:45 crossing from Newhaven to Dieppe. An absolute bargain, I seem to remember. Not only did it get me across the Channel, but it gave me a night's free accommodation, albeit a short one. And it got me to Dieppe in plenty of time to ride to the start so I could sign in the day before.

There is a wonderful cycle route from London to Paris called the *Avenue Verte*. Perhaps more wonderful in concept than in realisation, especially the English side. You have to admire the idea of a direct off-road route between these two great cities, one which makes the journey a pleasure, a recreational activity, a holiday experience that unites two great nations. Et cetera. In many places that is exactly what it is, but in others the idea has been diluted to a route on quiet roads more or less in the right direction. It does pass within a couple of kilometres from my house, though, and it was clearly a good place to start with my route-planning. A lot of it was on footpaths and bridleways out of London that I knew would be more trouble than they were worth, especially given that I was going to be riding on a Friday evening, so my own version (see map) missed this out and took the more direct roads out to Sutton and Banstead. And then after Gatwick, the *Avenue Verte* went in a ridiculous loop, and this on minor roads, and I could see a perfectly good bridleway that went much more directly over the final 10km to Newhaven. The first of these deviations was a good idea.[50]

I set off at two in the afternoon and MGL took a photo as I left, as she did two years earlier when I rode to the start of LEL, the big difference being that neither of us had to be up before dawn to do it.[51] It felt wrong to be departing mid-afternoon, as if early morning is the only proper time to set off on a long journey.

It was a pleasant ride to begin with. There was little time pressure, as the ferry was the late one and I already had a ticket. I was aiming to get to Newhaven early enough I wouldn't have to navigate bridleways in the dark, and so that I'd have time for a decent meal when I got

---

[49] Both Audax UK and Paris Brest Paris have their own Facebook pages.

[50] In retrospect, the bridleway, although it caused me some stress at the time, was worth the diversion both in terms of saving time, albeit not very much time at all, and in terms of having something to talk and write about.

[51] Another difference is that the photo, a beautifully composed picture that shows the author's enviable athleticism, seems to have been lost.

there. I expected to get lost a little, but the first couple of hours were good. I passed Coulsdon and crossed the North Downs and the M25 both near Godstone, and travelled south on minor roads that were roughly parallel with the A22, intersecting with this main road at East Grinstead and Forest Row, where I ate a felafel sandwich, and finally just beyond Uckfield, when I headed due south for Newhaven. The roads were beautifully quiet on a beautiful sunny evening. I passed close by Glydebourne, the Sussex country home of opera before coming to the town of Glynde, where I had brought Junior once for a camping adventure. From there, the road crossed the A27, with a dead end sign that I completely ignored. After that, there was a lovely single track road that led steeply up onto the South Downs as the sun was setting. I could not believe my luck.

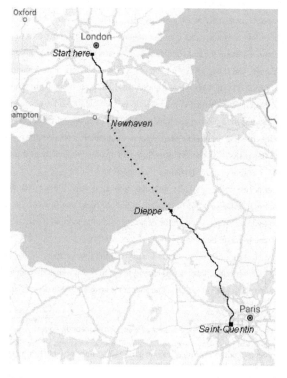

How I got to Paris

I was in the mood for adventure. I was riding a line I had seen on a map, a line representing a road that had existed since long before there were motor cars in England and that was fading into disuse. I was riding a bike I'd had built to take me on just such a road and I was carrying a bare minimum of luggage for a week of travelling. I had cycled half the day, and I was nearing the end of my day's journey. I could sense the sea ahead of me, even if I wasn't sure I could smell it yet.

The road grew steeper, but I had the gears for steep hills. The sun had gone and the heat drained away from the day, but the uphill climbing kept me warm. There was a threat of rain in the air but I carried waterproofs.

The road, which was already barely wide enough for a single car, narrowed. As it narrowed, its surface began to surrender itself to gravel. It continued uphill. I stopped, less certain than I had been fifteen minutes before, wanting to check the map on the screen of my phone, and unable to do this while riding since, although the phone was anchored to my handlebars, my handlebars would not remain still enough for me to study it.

The line on the map was still there, although now it was a dashed line that meant bridleway. A bridleway is a route designated for horses in particular, and permitted for cyclists and pedestrians, although permitted does not mean necessarily easy or indeed possible. There are some bridleways you would want to be a very competent horse rider for, and to be riding a very surefooted horse. I have learnt from several mistakes that I tend to be far more confident about the suitability of bridleways when sitting at a computer planning a ride than when I am actually on one.

The line existed on Pocket Earth, but it did not exist on GoogleMaps. While looking at GoogleMaps though, I was able to see that any alternative route meant considerable back-tracking and then the same circuitous route around to Newhaven I had rejected previously. In all likelihood the best bet would be to continue the way I had chosen and make the best of it.

Getting back on the bike, to continue up an incline on a gravel surface, I found it difficult to get my feet located in the pedal cleats with my new shoes. As I may have mentioned. Difficult in this case means in particular that several times one foot skidded off the pedal so that I cracked my ankle or my shin on the hard metal of crank or pedal.

The road that was no longer a road but a bridleway gave up all pretence of hard surface and became an overgrown path across fields of grass. In the dusk, it was differentiated mostly by the texture of the grass, and by a fence on one side, and something of a ridge, perhaps a couple of inches in height, on the other. You could tell that occasionally a farmer drove a Land Rover or a tractor along here, and that the fields on either side would be much harder going.

The grass was long and if it hadn't been combed flat by the wind, my wheels would have disappeared into it. As it was, I had to trust there were no chasms hidden by the grass that would sink me.

I reached a summit and could see, all at once, the dark sea beyond the darkening country, and the lights of the town and the ferry port, and the clearly defined footpath, the South Downs footpath, it had to be, crossing my route from left to right.

It had begun to rain some time ago and I stopped to put on my GoreTex. The route ahead was still a grassy path between grassy meadows.

I went on. The downhill path steepened, and I needed my brakes. It steepened more, and I could feel ruts under my front wheel, and I needed not only my brakes but all my concentration.

And suddenly my front wheel disappeared from under me and I was down on the ground, still astride my bike, my shoulder hard on the ruts of the path. I had no idea how it had happened.

I got up. Levelled the bike, and set off again. And instantly fell flat, my shoulder banging on the ground.

My first thought, once I knew I was not hurt, was that the bike was irrevocably bent out of shape. Unridable. The handlebars seemed to be angled impossibly. I got to my feet again, very gingerly, and looked at the bike, leaning to one side and then to the other to assess it properly. Other than a stripe of mud on the down tube, nothing wrong with it.

But the wheel slipped from under me again, the third time in the space of a minute, and this time I was alert enough to see how it happened. Here the grass of the bridleway was worn away to reveal the chalk beneath, wet with the rain, and as slippery as ice.

I walked the next mile, carefully minding my loaded bicycle down the steep hill, brakes on, elated that nothing was wrong with it. Eventually the gradient lessened, and as it did, as if an evil spell was lifted, the rain eased away, the meadows gave way to woods, and the track picked up tarmac once again. I mounted the bike, put my lights on, and freewheeled gently towards Newhaven. Quickly the tarmac path widened to be a road, one permitting cars not only in one direction but in two, with white lines painted to separate them. Scarcely had it done that, the road ended at a T junction with the A26, where signposts told me it was 57 miles to London and only one to Newhaven.

I followed my nose and my GPS route to the bright arc lights of the ferry port. In the midst of the huge space and the bright lights, there was a small low building in which I found a woman behind a desk to whom I could present my ticket, and a place to wait. I had hoped for a café, a good meal and much tea, and perhaps the company of a band of other cyclists to while away the hours before the ship sailed. There was no café, no meal and no tea, but there was a cyclist sitting on a plastic chair.

He was clearly an audaxer. A white man in his fifties, the most common demographic. As am I. He was wearing a red cycle jersey and looked like he had cycled from somewhere to be here. I asked him the obvious questions and he answered yes to the ferry and to PBP, and we chatted for a while. His name was Peter. He'd taken the train down from Preston to London, but he'd cycled from London, travelling a more sensible route than me and successfully arriving before it got dark, which was already over an hour ago. We had a couple more hours to wait for the ferry.

I had some emergency food with me, in the event of there being no café available, and so did Peter, so we could eat. In addition, I could text MGL and could catch up with Facebook (which doesn't take me very long).

More cyclists arrived, half a dozen of them in one group, then an older couple. The group were doing a sponsored cycle from London to Paris, the older couple were on a touring holiday. Then a second group of audaxers. Eventually it was time to go outside and wait instead of waiting inside. The ferry was there, massive and dark in the night. The cars and lorries it had brought over from France had all gone, but nothing was being loaded yet. There was more waiting.

Men and women in fluorescent jackets moved around. It wasn't clear what was going on, but I was too lazy to ask. I assumed that some time before the ferry was due to depart somebody would direct cars and such onto the boat, and so it proved. The bikes were to go on last, so we dozen or so cyclists clustered around their bikes in a corner of the waiting area and watched the fluorescent jackets organise the traffic. Finally it was our turn.

I got shouted at for cycling onto the boat. Apparently you had to walk the bike, as somebody had decided that was a safer option. That somebody had clearly never seen cyclists wearing cleats trying to wheel loaded bicycles over a wet metal surface, and nobody had bothered to tell them.

In the hold most of the cyclists, myself included, locked our bikes. One of the crew was laughing at us.

"I don't know who you think is going to take them."

I suppose he had a point, and cycle theft at sea is not often reported, but habits die hard.

I climbed upstairs on the ship to the passenger decks. Other cyclists were already staking out places to sleep, comfortable quiet corners where they were unlikely to be disturbed, or at least minimally uncomfortable places where nobody would actually trip over them. I did the same. The best place was a play pen with a nice padded floor, a low, padded, perimeter wall, and a sign saying "No Adults Allowed". Since I am rather a timid soul, the sign was enough to deter me. The second-best place was a carpeted stretch underneath the stairs that led up to the upper passenger deck, a small space only really big enough for two and already occupied by two girls with rucksacks. I found a patch of wooden floor and laid out my sleeping bag. Others did the same around me.

Of course it was possible to book a cabin and travel in style, although it was a lot of money to pay for five hours in a bed, and contrary to the spirit of the thing, at least in my eyes.

At five in the morning, awoken by the roar of the ferry's engines turning the boat about to dock in port, I crawled reluctantly out of my sleeping bag and stowed it in my pannier. There were a good number of fellow sleepers doing the same, although those who had chosen the play pen were so comfortable there they were still asleep. A little later, somewhat tired and bewildered, I followed a dozen other cyclists and rode off the suddenly empty ferry and onto French soil. Everything was either pitch black or bright lights, the lights both the high flooding arc lamps of the ferry port and the darting LEDs of my fellow riders, red and white.

The LEDs were more red than white since I was almost the last on the road, having faffed a little to get my phone set up with the Pocket Earth app and its display of the *Avenue Verte* in all its glory pointing towards Paris. The red lights moved away from me, a peloton of eager riders with 200km in front of them. To be honest I was happy to have my own space, and to enjoy the cool of the night and breathing fresh air after the stale warmth of the ferry interior. In any case, having researched the *Avenue Verte*, I wanted to explore it, and was wary of following other cyclists in case they took me on a route that diverged wildly from my own.

The road off the ferry quickly became the D1 and I could see from the screen of my phone that this road not only led all the way to Paris but that it ran largely parallel to the *Avenue Verte*, and crossed and re-crossed it frequently, at least in the first few dozen miles. At five in the morning, the D1 was gloriously empty and well-surfaced, and it was an easy decision to stick to this road until daylight.

Dieppe disappeared into countryside surprisingly rapidly, as the red rear lights of other cyclists disappeared ahead of me, and I had the road to myself.

There was no wind, and moon enough for me to see the road in front. The poor-quality sleep I had had on the ferry was good enough I felt refreshed, so that when the road rolled upwards to Martin-Eglisse I didn't really mind. I enjoyed the ride in the early morning, and happily occupied myself comparing the road and the *Avenue Verte* on my phone map, watching the little ▲ that represented myself on the screen moving on one side of the blue route line and then on the other.

Gradually it grew lighter, the sky brightening to my left, and at the same time it began to dawn on me I was hungry. This was poor timing on my part, because anything remotely edible had long been consumed, and every town I rode through offered a selection of unlit and very much not-open shops.

With the light came a little traffic. A car every other minute or so, then perhaps two cars in a minute, and it was time for me to investigate the off-road route.

It was easy to find, there were blue signposts to it at frequent intervals, and, following one, I was there, turning left onto a cycle path that clearly had once been the line of a railway. The surface was good pavement, not so smooth as the road, but the lack of traffic more than made up for that. Every mile or two it passed the remaining superstructure of what had been a village railway station. Occasionally there was a café, closed at this time of the morning.

I passed a group of cyclists loitering around one of these cafés. I didn't doubt for a moment that they had been on the same ferry and were cycling to the same destination as myself, and they wished me good morning in English as I went past. Ten minutes later they passed me, moving at speed, riding with the discipline of the race peloton.

The route was pretty flat, as most railway lines and former railway lines are, and peaceful without being dramatic in terms of scenery. Perfectly pleasant, but I had a nagging sense that if I could stop for a coffee and a croissant then I would be getting more of the authentic French experience. So on the approach to every town, I was looking for any indication of a nearby café, studying both the LED map on my handlebars and the signposts along the route. Several times, with what was, in hindsight, a very naïve sense of optimism, I took a detour and followed a road that promised a village centre, but in each case I failed to find such a centre, or I failed to find a shop in it, or I failed to find a shop that was open. One of these towns was Neufchâtel-en-Bray, famous, I now learn, for heart-shaped soft cheese. Of course, sadly I was there too early for it to provide me with said cheese or any other material of sustenance. Finally I came to the town of Forges-les-Eaux and it was eight o'clock in the morning and there was a busy little town centre and a pretty café in front of a crossroads with half a dozen bicycles leaning against the wall outside. The same crew who had passed me earlier.

I hadn't been particularly cold while cycling, but the café was very cosy and welcoming. I ordered *café au lait* and a croissant and enjoyed this enough to order a second *café au lait*, and had been sitting there for three quarters of an hour before I was able to move.

After Forges-les-Eaux the *Avenue Verte* ran out of disused railway and had to continue on minor roads, which was okay because it was early on a Saturday morning in August and the roads were quiet. The wind was gentle and it was pleasant riding.

As the morning wore on, however, the roads became busier, and there was a creeping urbanisation as I got closer to Paris. Just after I passed through the town of Gisors, my route departed from the *Avenue Verte*, since, although I was intending to ride Paris Brest Paris, the event didn't start in Paris on the *Champs Elysess* or at the Eiffel Tower but in a small new town near Versailles. After Gisors I caught up with Peter from Preston and we cycled together.

We agreed that we were both hungry, and started looking for feeding opportunities, fully expecting that the increasing urbanisation would be equated with such opportunities. We did see a McDonalds, but neither of us were prepared to stoop that low.

The route I had planned on my computer at home seemed to have us passing through a continuously urban area without ever going through town centres. I was confident of my route enough that I didn't even have a map with me, and Peter was in a similar situation except that he couldn't get his GPS to work so had to rely on me for directions.

At one point we took a diversion off the main road in what seemed to be a promising direction and came to a large and shambolic market, which included a number of street cafés providing food of many ethnicities. Peter seemed distinctly uncomfortable, and was very much against stopping, so I picked up some fruit instead, thinking it would do me until I found something more luxurious. Without a map, neither of us wanted to deviate much from the one GPS route we had between us, and we didn't see anything tempting enough at the roadside. We obviously weren't really hungry.

We arrived at the National Velodrome in the suburb of Saint-Quentin-en-Yvelines in the early afternoon. Peter went to find his hotel, but I had no hotel to find and gravitated towards the crowd of cyclists that swarmed around the gates. It was all very confused; even the cyclists who knew what was going on acted as if they didn't.

In such a situation, it is only that part of the crowd close enough to the front to ask questions and to hear answers who know what is going on. In the friendly, almost festival, noisiness, the distance over which questions and answers were possible was only a couple of metres. On the other hand there is such a thing as a swarm mentality, and the swarm knew it was flowing—chaotically, but flowing nonetheless— through the gates and into the gardens and grounds surrounding the velodrome.

I wasn't supposed to have my bike checked until 4 o'clock, but with nothing better to do, I was going with the flow. By the time I reached the entrance, and a volunteer in a hi-vis jacket pointed for me to proceed, it would have been near impossible to do anything else. I followed 'a lane marked by temporary barriers to arrive at the back of a queue of men and women with bicycles. I am an Englishman; I understand queues.

The queue ended in the shade of a row of gazebos, and now it was like entering a new country in the sense you had to present your passport or ID as well as registration documents. The officials[52] here, after they had checked the paperwork, would direct you to a second line of officials, one of whom would look your bicycle over to check that it adhered to the safety guidelines. This last bit was like going through customs, although it was not so much the absence of drugs or commercial quantities of alcohol or cigarettes that was required but the presence of two working brakes (or one front brake and a fixed wheel) and working lights front and rear. The printed regulations also required reflectors on the pedals, which I now remembered had generated some discussion on cycling forums, since most modern clipless pedals are designed without such reflectors. Fortunately, and this confirmed a suspicion I have long held about French society and regulations, nobody was checking pedal reflectors.

But they *were* checking lights, and I was both surprised and disappointed that my bike failed in this regard. The rear light failed to illuminate itself, let alone anything else, even when the front wheel and therefore the front wheel dynamo was spinning. Clearly a wire had come loose. And recently. I was sure the light had been working during the evening when I was cycling to the ferry. I could only imagine that while it was stacked with other bicycles on the ferry somehow the connection to the rear light had become dislodged. Otherwise it must have been when I was falling off the bike or carrying it over rough ground on my bridleway route into Newhaven. Either way, I had been cycling before the dawn out of Dieppe without a rear light.

I had a small battery rear light with me, and showing this to the volunteer enabled me to obtain a stamp on my registration documents and a sticker on my frame certifying my bike as roadworthy. But I didn't want to rely on my emergency battery lamp, so I spent the next 20 minutes making the necessary repairs. On finding the broken connection, unfortunately it was

---

[52] Unlike the situation you meet at border controls, it is only fair to point out that the officials here were volunteers, and they shared a passion for cycling.

not a simple as reconnecting it; the wire was no longer long enough for that, and I had to remove it from its aesthetically-satisfying, invisible route inside the rear mudguard to make a less attractive shortcut along the mudguard stay.

This achieved, I could park the bike and go inside the velodrome to pick up my brevet card and other goodies.

Upon presentation of my stamped registration document, the security officers on the door of the velodrome let me inside. These men looked very serious, which made getting in seem all the more special. Inside, it was crowded with excited people, a whole babble of noise, and the excitement was infectious. The beautiful wooden boards of the cycle track went around the outside, and inside, it was like some kind of exhibition with a big unruly queue of people working its way towards various stands. Actually several queues, all of them converging on a line of tables loaded with cardboard boxes. Most of the cardboard boxes were labelled with a small plastic flag denoting relevant countries, or at least languages.

I saw one of the stalls advertised London-Edinburgh-London and went over to talk to organiser Daniel Webb and filmmaker Damon Peacock. I mentioned to the latter that I'd seen the video clip he'd posted which included a scene showing me bravely peddling through the morning during the Mersey Roads 24, while his benevolent voice-over spoke of slower riders remaining overdressed. I joked that I was upset. He recognised me as Mr Four Minutes – I'm

on his LEL video being interviewed after arriving within four minutes of my time limit of 116 hours. I bought a copy of the aforementioned LEL DVD, knowing how much MGL would appreciate watching it. Then I browsed at a couple of other stalls — fancy bicycles, clothing, other stuff, before I joined the queue behind the British flag.

The multiple queues were, shall we say, informal, but they were good-natured, and I made it through the melee to pick up the following items:

- the all-important brevet card
- a tracking chip on a Velcro strap to go around my ankle
- a badge with my entry number to go on my bike frame
- a badge with my entry number to go on my helmet
- a ticket for the jersey I had ordered
- a ticket for the reflective vest that came free with my entry

The tracking chip had to be worn at all times, a bit like those tags they give to hooligans on ASBOs. It would automatically register the time I arrived at every control, and the idea was that this time would be available to my loved ones tracking me on the internet. The badges were important because the official photographers would need to be able to identify each rider from their photograph for the purposes of selling those photographs. I dutifully stuck mine on; I never managed to remove the one on the helmet.[53]

With the last-mentioned tickets, I joined another queue in front of another line of tables, this one not differentiated by country. Language problems here were bypassed by everybody simply waving their tickets in the air until a volunteer would swap one for an item in a see-through plastic bag. In this way I received my hi-vis reflective vest, which was to change the way I saw night-time cycling gear (pun intended), and the hilarious commemorative Paris-Brest-Paris 2015 cycle jersey.

At least, I found it hilarious.

Having overheard somebody saying there were facilities available, I went to have a shower. As you might expect in a sports arena, the toilets and changing rooms are underneath the stands. Leaving the main area, passing underneath the track, I quickly found myself walking up and down empty staircases and corridors, something made all the more entertaining by my choice of footwear, namely the new sporty cycle shoes with the hard, non-stick soles that not

---

[53] For reasons that will become apparent later in this book, it became necessary to replace my helmet before the end of the year.

only make every step a slightly hit or miss affair, but also made great echoes with the hard surfaces all around.

The official PBP 2015 shirt. On the front is Paris's Eiffel Tower, on the back the Phare du Petit Minou in Brest, potent symbols both. Neither iconic building features on the route.

The shower, after cycling to Newhaven, (90km), sleeping in my cycling gear on the boat, and then cycling to Paris (170km), was very welcome, even with my comedy small towel and having to rummage through my panniers to find clean cycle shorts and a vest.

That done, I was free to find some nightlife. And necessarily, something to eat.

Saint-Quentin-en-Yvelines is a new town of about 150 000 people, not overly far from Versailles. It is one of the original five *villes nouvelles* of Paris and was named after the Saint Quentin lake, which was chosen to become the town's centre. The town was built from a green-field site starting in the 1960s. Like many other new towns, it is somewhat soulless. Largely made up of multistorey concrete buildings, it reminded me of Canary Wharf as much as any-thing, and when I rolled my bicycle the half-mile downhill to the centre, or what I took to be the centre, the bars and restaurants seemed to be very much like those around a financial dis-trict. There may be a shopping mall, and schools, playgrounds, health centres and other aspects of civilisation commensurate with a town, but I did not find them. Anyway, bars and restaurant were my immediate concern.

The bars and restaurants seemed to be crowded with cyclists; there were bicycles parked everywhere, and most of the people sitting at tables outside were wearing the kind of clothes more usually associated with cycle sport than with a Saturday night on the town.

Crowded though places were, I did not feel so much like a stranger in a strange town. The people here, although I did not know them, were of my own tribe. It was not a problem to sit down at a table already occupied, order a beer, and join in a conversation.

In this way I met a bunch of Irish cyclists, most of them in green, who had flown into Paris that morning and made their way around the city to get here. When they left, I was working on my second beer and my pizza had arrived. Behind me two Americans, David and Alec, were having a lively conversation about miles and kilometres in the context of cycling, and litres and pints in the context of drinking. I found myself drawn into the conversation, and was soon sitting with them and enjoying their camaraderie. I drank more than I meant to drink, but it was still early by the time I left the bar. Not quite dark.

My plans, as far as accommodation was concerned, were a little tenuous. There was a campsite close to the velodrome, and I thought that would make a backup plan, even though I was unable to ascertain whether or not it permitted tents or bivvy bags. I was hoping I would be able to bed down in the grounds of the velodrome, but when I returned there, I found the gates locked and purposeful-looking security guards standing inside. On the off chance, I checked with them if it was possible for me to come inside. They were very friendly, but not to the point of allowing me to trespass.

I cycled around the immediate vicinity, looking to see if there was a comfortable-looking place to lay out my bivvy bag. By comfortable I meant a place where I could feel secure enough to sleep without worrying about either my personal safety or my bike being nicked. Finding nothing, I went to the campsite.

The campsite reception was closed, all the lights out. I cycled in. The site was enormous, but only about three quarters full, and the pitches seemed to have been allocated in such a way that all those close to the entrance, and to the various facilities, had been taken, and all the empty ones were at the back, where there was no street lighting on the driveways. I did a little tour of the campsite, being both curious as to what there was, and indecisive about where I would sleep. Most of the campers were in enormous RVs, with a very small minority of caravans and large frame tents. I did see one smaller tent with a Quest velocipede[54] parked beside

---

[54] A quest is a long journey looking for something. A Quest velocipede is a recumbent tricycle with a full fairing to keep its rider protected from the elements. It has two wheels at the front and one at the back, so it is stable, and it parks like a (very) small car. It has lights, and a decent amount of storage space, so it can be used as a zero-emissions utility vehicle. But the real story is the fairing cuts air resistance down to the extent a reasonably fit rider can easily average 50km/h. Admittedly that's on flat roads. Uphill, you have to carry the weight of the fairing, and such a vehicle also loses all the advantages of a bike in traffic. And a Quest will cost as much as a decent secondhand car. But they

it, but this was the exception rather than the rule. Eventually, I chose a place on an empty pitch adjacent to places with tents and camper vans and people. Thinking it was possible somebody would drive an enormous campervan onto the pitch in the middle of the night, I set up the bivvy bag so close to a tree that it would be impossible for even the most tired and unobservant driver to run me over. At least by accident. I locked the bike on one side of the tree and lay down on the other, inside layers of Lycra, silk, down-filled nylon, and Gore-Tex, and once I had wriggled myself into an approximately comfortable position, I fell asleep.

have the wow factor. I want one, and when the sales of this volume make me a millionaire, I shall put in my order.

CHAPTER ELEVEN

The First Day

I woke up just after dawn, with a giant campervan carefully reversing into the pitch on which I had been asleep. One man was driving the van, and another was directing him. Both were aware of my presence, and didn't seem to be bothered by it. On the other hand the close proximity of a big diesel engine, and the admittedly quiet excitement of a family arriving for their summer holiday, made for a pretty good alarm clock. The man who had just directed his brother's van wished me *bonjour* and indicated I should continue to sleep if I wanted. I did try.

A little later the man from the campsite came and asked me where my car was. My communication powers in French not particularly enhanced through my being semiconscious, my attempt to persuade him that I had no car seemed to give him the impression that I was with the family in the adjacent pitch and had decided to sleep outside for the peace and quiet. He approved of this with a grin. I went back to sleep, realising I had missed my opportunity to pay for my night's accommodation.

By about 8 o'clock I had dressed, rolled up my sleeping kit, put my cycling shoes on, and returned to the velodrome, happy to find the gates open and a few people inside. I parked the bike, selecting a place where my advertisement was prominent, and laid out the damp bivvy bag over a fence to dry before visiting the coffee van parked prominently in the middle of the gardens.

Frank and Berry from Denmark were looking at my bike. My bike, as I may have mentioned, is a joy and a delight and a midlife crisis to me. It is also somewhat questionable, in the sense that many cyclists have questions to ask about it. For example: is that a motor you've got there?[55] What's that lump on the end of your handlebars?[56] Is it heavy?[57]

Frank and Berry were eating cakes. Small round sticky chocolaty cakes. It turns out the cakes are called Paris Brests. "They are named after the cycle event," Frank told me.

I chatted with them about cycling and rain and sunshine and hard kilometres and easy kilometres and then I went to buy myself a cup of coffee and a Paris Brest.

To be honest, the cake was a little bit disappointing. Too sweet. Perhaps after five hours in the rain and in the saddle (me, not the cake), I would like them more.

The coffee van was a vintage Citroën and in front of it were six metal tables with matching chairs for coffee-drinking cyclists to sit in the sunshine and enjoy the ambience. I did that, enjoying the coffee and the sunshine until I had no more coffee and felt it was probably time to let somebody else have the chair.

I rearranged my luggage, my sleeping bag, and what minimal non-cycling clothing I had into a large plastic bag which I took to the left luggage facility. I would ride PBP with two small panniers and my handlebar bag, not as much as a touring cyclist would carry, but more than most people on this ride. Unlike most riders, I did not have any accommodation booked and didn't expect to be relying on using mattresses at the controls.

---

[55] My beloved bicycle has a Rohloff hub gear, which contains 14 evenly spaced gears inside the rear wheel. This exotic German technology comes at a price, but is famously low-maintenance and long-lived, which is why I bought mine second-hand. A colleague of mine has just bought an electrically assisted bicycle, with a motor concealed inside a hub which is a similar size to the Rohloff.

[56] The Rohloff is operated by a simple, reliable, and inelegant oversized gear knob.

[57] Yes.

I met Marcus JB. He was sitting on a step with a number of Audax Club Hackney members, most of whom supported fearsome beards. I thanked him for writing his list.

There was time to kill. It was only nine o'clock in the morning and I didn't start until five. I wandered around, admiring bicycles, having conversations with people I knew, and with people I didn't. I went into the town and bought some food to consume. I sat down in the sun and had a snooze.

At one o'clock, the first group of riders set off. For this occasion there were speeches and official photographs, and a commentator for the benefit of all. He was only speaking French, but he did this with sufficient excitement to carry a certain message across to speakers of all languages. As the time approached, a crowd gathered itself around the barricades erected to keep it away from the riders. I got close enough to have a good look.

This first group of riders, those whose bikes and helmets had labels starting with the letter A, were a fearsome-looking bunch. Hard-core. Some of them you would cross the road to avoid on a moderately dark evening. None of them had anything you would call luggage, and many did not bother with helmets. Most of them seemed to be pressed as far forward as was possible in their starting pen, anticipating the end of the countdown as you would the beginning of the race. For many of them it was a race. Riders in the A and B groups had committed themselves to completing the course in 80 hours, ten fewer than the rest of us, and selection for the first group would be on the basis of times on the qualifying rides.

They left at speed, very much as a peloton. Some of them would be back within 48 hours.

For me there was more waiting. Groups of about 50 riders were set off every 15 minutes, and I had time to kill while the event organisers worked from group A through to M. After the first two groups came the group of "specials", that is those riding velocipedes or tandems or something like that. Then it was the turn of the mere mortals who were expecting the full benefit of 90 hours to ride the distance, and the starts were more low-key. For every group of riders there was a little speech both in English and in French, mostly about obeying traffic regulations and such, then the riders were waved off, there was a measure of polite applause, and that was it.

I moved away from my viewing point and continued chatting with Frank and Berry for a while, and then I found a bit of shade and had another snooze, making some recompense for two successive nights of less than seven hours shut-eye. I whiled away the afternoon with a mixture of sleeping, eating, chatting and generally soaking up the atmosphere. It wasn't difficult.

By six o'clock I was dressed in what I would be wearing for the start, and I had the rest of my gear organised on the bike, including my GoreTex jacket and my reflective Paris Brest Paris 2017 gilet, both conveniently at hand for when it was cold and dark. I rolled down the slope to where we had had the machine check, now refashioned as the pre-start waiting area. As the time approached, we were corralled back up around to the starting pen. I listened to the same speech I had listened to and half-listened to several times already, curious to see how much of the French I could understand, and yet remembering almost nothing of the content. It was something like a weather forecast in that regard. There was a photograph just before the start, and a series of photographs as we set off. Naturally enough, all these photographs were, and probably still are, available for purchase, but the pictures in this book are sourced from elsewhere.

According to the device I had Velcroed to my ankle, it was 18:31 when we set off. The first stage was 140km in length, and early evening is an odd time to start such a long ride, you might think. On reflection it is certainly not ideal, and yet I actually chose my start time on advice, possibly Marcus's. I think the point of starting in the evening was that I would be in the middle of the mass of 6000 riders, and could therefore expect to see the biggest crowds along the way. The full experience. Anyhow, some night riding was unavoidable. And it is something I'm quite fond off. The disadvantages are about a lack of sleep. I would find out.

The Route of PBP 2015

I quickly struck up a conversation with two Americans, Bryan from North Carolina and Patrick from New Jersey. Being Americans, they were randonneurs rather than audaxers, and had different accents, and a different style of cycle clothing, favouring a more retro look involving wool. I would find out that less laid-back American cyclists, those who would consider themselves more sporty, favour Lycra.

I could tell Patrick was from New Jersey because he had the words "New Jersey" emblazoned on his top. For my benefit, Bryan asked Patrick what he would do when his New Jersey jersey was worn out.

"I'll have to buy myself a new New Jersey jersey," he said. An old joke. Patrick and Bryan were old friends.

The route took us around sidestreets of the new town, going around the lake but never close enough to see it, and then headed into the *parc naturel regional del la Haute Vallee de Chevreuse*, passing through the small town of Montfort-l'Amaury, and climbing up to almost 200m. The landscape was a mixture of arable farming and woodland, and gently rolling. The villages were small and pretty, and the streets were, as I'd hoped, lined with ordinary people cheering. Very early on, this riding experience made me feel heroic for simply riding a bicycle, and the enthusiasm of bystanders only increased as the event went on. On leaving the *parc naturel*, the landscape became slightly more arable and slightly less woodland. At Nogent-le-Roi, a lovely town on the River Eure, Patrick, Bryan and I took the first of what would be an excessive number of café stops. Up to that point we had covered 55km in reasonable, although not exactly fast, time.

We cycled on to Chateauneuf-en-Thymerais, by which time the road was rolling again, and then on to Senonches, where we entered another *parc naturel*, this one the *parc naturel du Perche*.

Le Perche is a former province of France which was split up into various departments during the French Revolution. The district is kind of defined by a semicircle of high ground to the west, which we would need to cycle over, and is famous for a breed of large and powerful horses called Percherons. A high proportion of immigrants to New France (i.e. Quebec) in the seventeenth century came from Perche and nearly all French-Canadians have ancestors here. The stage ended in the town of Mortagne-au-Perche, which at one time was the capital of the province.

Locals, according to the PBP website, are fond of saying that Mortagne is on the mountain, which is pushing it a bit at 260m, and when they are not saying that they say that it is the most beautiful village in France, something I am sure they are not alone in claiming. But it was dark by this time, so I couldn't be much of a judge. The stop here was not a control in the sense that there was any signing of the brevet card but otherwise it was a control. We were hosted, in the words of the website, by the Carré du Perche, which seemed to be a kind of Civic Centre. The promise was of food, bar and grill outdoors, sleeping and shower in the gymnasium and onsite parking. The eating area, I remember, was relatively small and crowded and predominantly orange in colour.

Patrick told me about something he called caffeine sleep. "What you do is this: you stop and drink a strong coffee. And then you lie down and sleep."

"Okay," I said, "if you're too tired to go on, you're too tired to go on."

"And then you wake up about fifteen minutes later."

"Because of the coffee."

"Exactly. And then you're ready. You've had fifteen minute's power nap, and the caffeine's just kicking in."

"I like that," I said, all-too-innocent.

So, as well as carbohydrates and tea, I drank a big cup of coffee, and then we found somewhere on the floor to lie down. This was easier said than done because most of the available space between chairs and tables had already been claimed by unconscious and semiconscious cyclists.

In the event, the food in our stomachs probably slowed down the process, and I think it was over an hour before we awoke.

Getting groggily to our feet, Patrick and Bryan and I located one another, consumed more coffee, and then made our way out into the night.

The second stage looped around the south of the town of Alencon, and covered 80km without ever bothering a town of significant size before reaching Villaines-la-Juhel. We passed through parts of the map shaded green for forest, most of this being the *parc natural regional Normandie-Maine*, none of which could really be seen in the darkness. The landscape remained gently, but persistently, rolling.

Gentle but persistent rolling was what we were doing. It was quiet at night, and we were going quietly except for the occasional burst of joking and laughter. Somewhere during the night Bryan lost contact with us. Patrick assured me he'd be fine, and clearly if he wasn't, there were hundreds of cyclists to give assistance. The majority of riders in these kinds of events aim to ride at their own pace; to ride faster than you want to, or to be waiting around for a companion who is too slow, is not only frustrating, but it can leave you overtired or cold.

And with so many cyclists going the same way, you are never at a loss for somebody to talk to.

We met Dawn, another American randonneur and a friend of Patrick's. She was easy to meet because from her handlebars came some rather ephemeral choral music, which was a surprising thing to meet in the dark lanes. Shortly after we met her, I had a puncture, rear wheel again, and we all stopped in a layby. Dawn made her excuses and left us, and Patrick held a torch to make my puncture-fixing experience easier.

We arrived in Villaines just after 6 o'clock on the morning of the 17th August, getting there when at last there was some light so we could see where we were. We stopped at the *Mairie*, or town hall, where the control was situated. Entering the control, we had to walk over a little footplate connected to a box of electronics. As you passed, there was a satisfying clunking sound as the system registered the sensor attached to your ankle. You went through to have

From left to right: Bryan, the author, Patrick, and Dawn. Selfie by Bryan

your brevet card signed, but in one way you were already clocked in.

There was a settlement in the area of the present day Villaines-la-Juhel from Roman times. In the middle ages there was a castle on raised ground in the centre of the town. It is documented that half the town was given to the monastery of St Marie in 692. In 1140, Matilda of England, whom I visited in chapter 2, gave the town to one Juhel II de Mayenne, in gratitude for services rendered, and the town achieved its full name from that day, although to locals it remains simply Villaines. It has been a control town for PBP since 1979.

Bryan arrived in time to join us for a very early breakfast, which in my case was lots of tea and comforting but forgettable carbohydrates. After eating, we sat around feeling sleepy, sometimes with eyes open, sometimes with eyes shut. We weren't the only ones, as you can see from this photograph.

An alternative view of the dining facilities at Villaines

CHAPTER TWELVE

To Brest

Stage three gave us 85km en route to Fougères, 309km in total, or about a quarter of the total distance we needed to cover.

Before reaching Fougères, we were riding on the same roads as the Tour de France the month before. These roads were still painted with professional riders' names and the decorations that communities had made were still there, decorations such as giant bikes, hay bales stacked up high with messages painted on them, bikes set up with dummies riding them, the dummies wearing the different leaders' jerseys, sign posts and flag banners, and messages painted on the sides of barns. Beside these were elaborate signs and banners made for the PBP riders. It was a special feeling to be sharing the road with the pros and have the crowds treat us with a similar welcome and encouragement.

After about 10km, the route turned north, crossing the busy N12 at Le Rebay and then heading back into the green-shaded area of the map. This was more of the *parc naturel régional Normandie-Maine*, and now that we could see it, it was an area of sandy ridges and vast forests. It was all very pleasant.

After just over an hour of cycling, certainly long enough for our bodies to have forgotten breakfast, the sight of a lovely café at Lassay-les-Châteaux, just a metre off the route, was too much to resist. And if it hadn't been, there was another Patrick sitting there, this one Whitaker, another American, and the friend of my two travelling companions. We enjoyed coffee and croissants, sitting in the morning sunshine in a leisurely fashion, as if we had all the time in the world. Eventually tearing ourselves away from the café after a second coffee, we headed westwards, gently, but without major stopping, to reach the next control at Fougères just before 1 o'clock in the afternoon.

The author, Bryan, Patrick and Patrick enjoying coffee.

I was with Patrick and Bryan still, moving at a steady but unhurried pace, certainly a pace that did not endanger conversation. It was good getting to know these people. They told me about the Adrian Hands and Charly Miller Societies, both American organisations associated with PBP.

The Société Adrian Hands was created in 2009 in order to honour Adrian Hands and like-minded cyclists. Adrian was an American randonneur who travelled far and wide to do his thing, including brevets in China and Bulgaria. He completed PBP in 2003 in a time of 88:55. In 2005, however, he was diagnosed with a neurodegenerative disorder, later determined to be motor neurone disease, which caused him to lose upper extremity strength to the extent that soon he was unable to ride a normal bike. He switched to a recumbent cycle and successfully qualified for PBP in 2007. He got as far as Loudeac during the return trip from Brest in 2007, but retired there after being severely delayed with a puncture he was unable to fix due to his condition. He died in 2011. Membership of La Société Adrian Hands requires a finish time of 88:55 or longer (i.e. between 88:55 and 90:00 hours)

Charly Miller of Chicago was the first American to ride Paris-Brest-Paris. He finished in fifth place in 1901, when the event was a race, completing the course in 56 hours, 40 minutes.

This time was an outstanding achievement for an unsupported rider, especially given the poor roads and heavyweight bicycles of that era, and his placing all the more so considering that many of his opponents had teams of pacers and helpers along the route. Miller overcame a disheartening number of punctures and a broken bicycle in order to finish, riding a hastily borrowed replacement bike for the last 330km. Membership of the Charly Miller Society is limited to riders who have completed PBP in 56:40 or better.

Charly Miller during PBP in 1901

Neither Patrick nor Bryan could tell me about anybody who is a member of both societies.

The control was in a high school, the Lycée Jean Guéhenno. Fougères is, according to the PBP website, true cycling land, and it is a town the event has visited from the beginning. It also featured in the Tour de France in 2013 and 2015. The town has many tourist attractions — a wonderful castle, a historic old town, and national forest nearby (I'm quoting the website again) — but we didn't hang around very long to do them justice.

It is frighteningly easy to fall asleep whilst driving a car, particularly at night when the view through the windscreen is fairly monotonous, and because modern cars are warm and comfortable. By contrast it is quite difficult to fall asleep on a bike, what with the air rushing past your face. At night, it's more difficult still because the air rushing past your face is cold. In any case, generally the moment you start to fall asleep, you stop pedalling, or at least slack right off, and as you slow down the bike becomes less stable. Eventually, it will tip over, but as it does so, it will lurch into the fall to regain its balance. The shock of such an event wakes you up, at least for a while, and you look where you are going, and correct it if the lurch has taken you sideways.

Writing this down, this aspect of long-distance cycling doesn't seem very safe. At one time, I would have disagreed. I actually failed to appreciate how it was even possible to fall asleep while cycling.

A couple of years ago, riding LEL, as described in that other book which I have promised to stop plugging, I'd had a conversation with a tricyclist who had confessed to falling asleep twice previously. On the third occasion this particular tricyclist rode his trike into the back of a stationary car and was hospitalised. Of course on a tricycle, you don't lose your balance, and this, I thought, was a crucial difference.

At one stage during the afternoon, the odometer display of my cycle computer showed 5733.6km and my blurred vision somehow registered the numbers as reading "SLEEP". Do try. If you half-close your eyes you might be able to see it. That my cycle computer was advising me to sleep was confusing in itself; not only was there the question of how the numerical display could communicate in words, but of how such a simple device could so accurately analyse my state of health. When I managed to focus my eyes enough to read the numbers I was perplexed as to how I could have misled them, and that confusion helped me just a little and just for a while.

I was riding with Patrick at the time. When he recognised that I was sleepy he introduced me to the alphabet game. Of course when he explained it, it was very familiar, it's something I've had to play on long car journeys with my son. One player names an example of a category, for example an animal or a capital city or a football team. The other player then has to name another example of the same category that begins with the last letter of the first example.

For example:

"Lion."

"Newt."

"Tiger."

"Rattlesnake."

"Elephant."

"Trout."

"Tadpole."

At which point you might make an objection, since a tadpole is not an animal in itself but only the juvenile form of the frog, which begins with an *F*. Since Patrick and I came from countries with a different interpretation of the word *football*, we gave football teams a miss and stuck to animals and capital cities mostly, but we did try out names of countries as well. Country names get difficult pretty quickly, because there are a whole lot of countries whose last letter is *a*, but only 11 start with that letter. With the benefit of the internet I can get Afghanistan, Albania, Algeria, Andorra, Angola, Antigua, Argentina, Armenia, Australia, Austria, and Azerbaijan. Relying on memory alone, and with less than 100% of mental faculties in operation, we missed Antigua and Armenia. One might note that nine of these countries actually end with the letter A as well.

Whilst this game might seem pretty lame, and it is difficult to imagine adults sitting around a dinner table or at a party playing it, it turned out to be a pretty good pastime whilst cycling through northern France on a sunny afternoon. Not only did it wake me up, but both of us were getting something of a buzz out of it.

Stage four was just over 50km but I took nearly 3 hours over it, rolling into Tinténiac at 4:10 in the afternoon. A speed of approximately 16 km/h can only be justified by mention of the distracting pleasures along the route. Here and there, families had put tables outside their homes offering refreshments, sometimes simply water, sometimes food, once very good coffee. Also a very decent café turned up at what seemed to be a perfect time for a late second lunch. There were riders who, motivated by achieving admirable average speeds and impressive times over the 1200km, were able to overcome such distractions, but I imagine I was in the majority who embraced them. I can resist everything except temptation.

If you draw a line on a map going due west from the town of Fougères then after about 50km you will reach the town of Tinténiac. If you then try to find a route along the roads closest to that line, you will have this stage of PBP 2015.

Tinténiac is a rural town with a population of 3000 dating back to at least 1032. (The town, not its population.) The Ille et Rance canal, which connects the Atlantic Ocean at Redon to the Channel at Dinard, flows through the town. Tinténiac and its cycling club l'Amicale Cyclotouriste d'Ille-et-Rance have hosted PBP since 1979 and so this was its tenth time. There were 150 volunteers working at the control, which was situated in the technical college there, the Lycee Bel Air.

One traditional dish from Brittany is the Glamorgan sausage, which is made with Caerphilly cheese. In Breton, it is called *Selsig Morgannwg*. That the dish has its origins in Wales under-lines the connections between the Celtic countries to the north west of Europe. Although nom-inally I am vegetarian, in extreme situations I find it very difficult to resist sausage.

Patrick, Bryan and I discovered them first in Tinténiac. We passed a café that was barbe-cuing them out on the street just before the control. I asked if we were going to stop.

"The control is just there," Bryan said.

"I am definitely hungry," Patrick said.

Nevertheless we went to the control and signed in, but when we saw significant queues for food there, we backtracked the hundred metres to the sausage source.

"It's important to eat," I said, watching the sausages sizzle on the grill, "or else you start bonking."[58]

The sausages were served in a bread roll, but they were big and cumbersome, and, despite the adhesive qualities of mustard and ketchup, the bread needed to be held tightly to avoid the possibility of the sausage escaping. Patrick in particular was having difficulties, since he still seemed to have his cycle helmet in one hand.

"I think Patrick is struggling with his sausage," I observed. My comments were not considered helpful.

We were invited inside the café to eat the sausages, and inevitably once there it would have been rude not to have a beer with them. We enjoyed more sausage-related humour much in the manner of teenagers, our only excuse being extreme tiredness.

I think I still had some beer left when I had finished the sausage so I needed to order another sausage. And then I had sausage left when I had run out of beer...

Stage five covered about 85km and we rode it during the late afternoon and early evening of Monday, 18th August. We set off out of Tinténiac, going westwards on the D20, a road so ruler-

---

[58] To cyclists, bonking is when you have run out of blood sugar, and physical strength suddenly drops to almost zero. The cure is generally some fast calories. A Snickers and a ten minute stop can have you back to almost full power right away. If the word has an alternative meaning, this is just unfortu-nate.

straight that it has to date back to Roman times. After about 12km we were on the D220, but as far as direction and straightness was concerned, it was the same road, and it delivered us to Quedillac. A few kilometres later we turned south, down to St-Meen-le-Grand, before turning westwards once more to pass through Meneac and La Trinité-Porhoët before reaching Loudeac at a 9:45 in the evening. Somewhere along the way we met up with Frank who joined with us. Since both Frank and Bryan are photographers by profession, they were soon talking lenses and film and digital and whatever.

Loudéac is located in the centre of Britanny, framed by the River Oust and the River Lié, in the words of the PBP website. Its proudest attraction is the futuristic Palais des Sports which resembles a 3-D mathematical model more than it does a building, But I didn't see this since we didn't pass it, and it was dark anyway, and my priorities were more basic than admiring architecture.

I knew I needed some sleep, and after eating, I looked for a good place to do that, while others continued on their way.

I found the sleeping facilities provided at the control. The mattress on the floor arrangement came at a cost of four euros, which wasn't a showstopper in itself, but there was a queue, and not only that but the queue was outside in the courtyard and it was a bloody cold place to stand. However, although I had left my sleeping bag and mat in left luggage at the velodrome, I had kept the bivvy bag with me for just such an eventuality. I bedded down like a well-provisioned tramp in the opposite corner of the courtyard, between a parked car and two other sleeping cyclists. I found some cardboard to use instead of my inflatable mat, and with all my clothes on I was warm enough to get a few hours' sleep.

I woke up just after 3 o'clock in the morning. It was still night, but I was too cold to keep sleeping. I had had less than five hours' sleep, but I knew I could not afford much more at this stage in any case. I didn't bother to do the calculations, but I was not very much faster at the moment than the minimum average speed of 13⅓ km/h.

I drank some coffee and picked up a couple of croissants to eat on the way, and set off into the night, hoping that the dawn would soon appear behind me.

The route between Loudiac and Carhaix along the N164 is only about 60km, but our route instead crossed the main road and took a long detour to the north, along the smaller, and more demanding D roads. Whilst nothing like as hilly as Cornwall, this Gallic extremity of France contained more climbing than other parts of the event. In the darkness I couldn't see the hills,

115

which didn't help. Without being able to see an incline you can think it's just the pain in your legs playing tricks on you.

I stopped after just over an hour in the village of Saint-Martin-des-Prés, where a substantial temporary café had been built in a layby opposite the church. There were four or five trestle tables and bench seating for customers and another big table serving as the bar, and all this was under a row of gazebos. There was a man wearing an apron standing behind the bar, and, despite it being the dead of night, the place was still open for business. I wanted coffee. They had coffee. Perfect.

There were two other cyclists sitting under the canopies, almost invisible in the darkness. One seemed to be asleep, and the other nearly so. There was a very friendly atmosphere despite that everybody was so obviously weary. Even the guy in the apron had obviously been on his feet for a very long shift.

Leaving here, as the caffeine kicked in, I started off in the wrong direction. Fortunately there was a cry from behind me, *"Pas là-haut!"*

Other than answering calls of nature, I rode the rest of this stage without stopping. I was mostly on my own for the first time, only exchanging words with fellow cyclists when I caught them.

I approached Carhaix-Ploughuer in the department of Finistère as the sun rose, on what was to be a fine day. I had completed 525km in total with an average speed of 14.4 km/h. Although I had nearly three hours in hand, this wasn't much of a safety margin. I didn't stop for very long at this control, just time enough to find some breakfast, and then set off for Brest.

Carhaix is thought to be Carohaise of King Leodegrance in Arthurian legend. King Arthur apparently defended Leodegrance by defeating someone called Rience, and it was there he met Guinevere, who was Leodegrance's daughter. Carhaix is also identified with the Roman city of Vorgium, and archaeological digs have uncovered evidence of the ancient city, including its aqueduct system.

The *Fete des Vieilles Charrues* or Old Ploughs Festival held here every year in mid-July is not so much a celebration of ancient farm machinery but one of the largest music events in Europe, attracting more than 200,000 people. It is held in the fields once held by the *famille de* Saisy de Kerampuil, and the festival venue is next to the Chateau Kerampuil.

The name Finistère derives from the Latin Finis Terræ, which means the end of the earth, in a similar way to Cornwall's Land's End. The Shipping Forecast area of Finisterre was named after the Spanish equivalent, the peninsula at the westernmost point of Galicia. In 2002, the shipping area was renamed FitzRoy after Sir Admiral Robert FitzRoy who founded the Met Office in 1854. He was also, earlier in his career, captain of the Beagle which took Charles Darwin on his momentous five-year expedition around the world.

Stage 7, the stage that would take me to Brest, was 88km in length, and one of the most picturesque in the event. On a beautiful morning, the road now took me up into the *parc naturel regional d'Armorique*, 1200km² of protected rural land coloured green on the map, sweeping from the Atlantic Ocean into the hilly inland countryside.

Armorica is the name given to this part of the world in Roman times, that is, the part of Gaul between the River Seine and the River Loire, including the Brittany peninsular. The name comes from Gaulish for "place by the sea". The home village of comic-book hero Asterix the Gaul, where the "indomitable Gauls" hold out against the Roman Empire, is located in Armorica. On April Fools' Day in 1993, *The Independent* reported that Asterix's village had been discovered by archaeologists.

Between the fifth and seventh century there was a lot of immigration from Britain, and trade between Armorica and Britain goes back to long before the Roman period.

At the centre of the park, the *Monts d'Arrée* make up one of the oldest geological formations in Europe. Older than the Alps, they were created as mountains 600 million years ago, and have been ground down by wind and water ever since, to the extent that the highest hill, Tuchen Gador, is only 384m high. Nevertheless they marked the highest point on the PBP route, when the road passed by the television transmitter at *le Roc'h Trédudon* at 350m.

Monts d'Arrée is an area where Celtic mythology and Christian traditions coexist peacefully. A local legend explains why the Monts d'Arrée are so bare: when Christ was born, God asked the trees from the hills to cross the sea in order to greet the newborn child. All trees except for the humble pine, gorse and heather refused to do this, and so they were wrenched from the ground as divine punishment.

It was difficult to find the area so bleak as tradition would have it on such a sunny morning, and with the destination of Brest not so very far over the horizon. To make things even less bleak, I caught Alastair on the road up to the TV tower, the first I'd seen him since Wales.

Alastair had started at the velodrome a full hour after I had, but had clearly faffed around far less to make that time up in less than two days. We shared our impressions of the event so far, asking one another if it matched up to the expectations we'd held for it since riding LEL together two years ago. It did.

We came to the pretty town of Sizun, the discomfort of the cobbles in the town square easily compensated for by the cheers of the crowd, and we made a café stop on the Rue de Brest. Only 35km to go.

We crossed the estuary of the River Iroise on the *pont Albert-Louppe*. This bridge was built between 1926 and 1930 to connect the cities of Brest and Quimper. In 1944 the German army destroyed one arch of it to make it unusable by the Allied armies, and it wasn't until 1949 that the bridge was reopened. It was expanded in the 1960s, and by 1994 carried 28,000 vehicles per day, something it could not do without severe traffic congestion, and a new bridge was commissioned. That bridge, the cable-stayed *pont de l'Iroise*, with a central span of 400 m, is the third largest such bridge in France, and we had an excellent view of it from the *pont Albert-Louppe*, which is now reserved for non-motorised traffic.

We stopped to take photographs and admire the panoramic view of the town ahead of us; the harbours, the bay and the Goulet, a 3km long strait linking Brest to the Atlantic Ocean. It felt like we had arrived already, and I had a feeling of accomplishment, which was then seriously undermined by the ensuing miles and miles of urban cycling along the *rue de Quimper* before we eventually reached the control. The control was in the enormous educational campus of the district of Kerichen, *la cité scolaire de Kerichen*. It was 12:25 on a sunny afternoon, and we had travelled a distance of 614km in just over 40 hours.

The campus, with 4500 pupils and 500 teachers, is the size of a village, and contains three separate high schools and a college. In between the concrete buildings there is plenty of green space, and on the afternoon of the 18th August 2015 there were perhaps several hundred cyclists stretched out on the grass. One of them was Patrick. I found

him as we were wandering across the campus to the refectory which was set up to feed hungry cyclists. He was fast asleep, but when Alastair and I returned the same way having filled our faces, he was conscious. He'd got here about an hour before we did and didn't seem to be in any hurry to be anywhere else soon.

Patrick's bicycle required a little TLC, and I was happy to wait with him for a volunteer mechanic. In the meantime we admired the total wreckage of a bicycle frame beside the mechanic's stall and speculated as to how or if its rider would continue the event.

CHAPTER THIRTEEN

Going East

The first stage of the return journey, Stage 8, took us back to Carhaix, mostly on the same route as on the way out, but it avoided a second crossing of the bridge by taking us through the northeastern suburbs of Brest and the town of Guipavas. We re-crossed the River Elorn at Landerneau. Perhaps the most attractive feature of Landerneau is the sixteenth-century Rohan Bridge with slate-clad houses built upon it. The centre of this celebrated bridge is a pedestrian zone, so our route took us over the Pont de Moas Glas instead, which is much more utilitarian, and where the river is so unremarkable I barely noticed it.

Shortly after Landerneau, the route rejoined the road we had taken going west. Now, upon noticing cyclists coming the other way, we could feel a sense of superiority, since we were several hours ahead of them; they were going through something that was already in our past.

We passed through Sezun again, and back into the green part of the map, and the road rose single-mindedly up towards the peak at le Roc'h Tredudon.

There is a roundabout just before the TV transmitter, and there were a dozen or so spectators standing by it each time I passed. It was several kilometres from here to the nearest village. On the return journey I thought how remarkable this was, that a significant number of people had driven out to watch amateurs riding along a small part of the journey. It made me feel that what we were doing was special, that if ordinary people were prepared to celebrate it, we must be part of something worthwhile.

We started seeing what I jokingly referred to as X-men. These guys had registration numbers that started with an X, and they left at 5 o'clock in the morning, the day after the rest of the riders, and had to finish within 84 hours, instead of our 90. Not surprisingly, they were going faster than I was. Later on there would be Y-men as well, but that didn't have the same ring to it[59].

In the late afternoon, the route diverged from Stage 7 again, staying on the D754 all the way to Carhaix rather than remaining within the green-on-the-map *parc natural*. This more direct route was still scenic and rolling, just slightly less scenic and less rolling. The out and back routes conjoined once again shortly before Carhaix.

It was a pleasant afternoon's ride at a relaxed pace through beautiful scenery, and Alastair and I rolled back into Carhaix in the very early evening. The stage had covered about 85km, making a total distance of 698km.

There was gourmet food available for the cyclists here. The fish looked so good I thought it deserved to be eaten with a glass of wine.

Eating dinner here, we got talking to Damon Peacock and Heather Swift. They were working on a documentary film about the event, and we talked about what was so good about PBP, which was mostly the phenomenal crowds and the sense of occasion, and what was not so good, which was mostly to do with organisation at the controls, and the delays often caused to riders. We agreed that some of this was simply due to the scale of the event, and unavoidable, but some of it could be improved by better organisation. One key difference between LEL and

---

[59] Records show there were 17 X-women and 13 Y-women as well, but I didn't see them. All but one of these 30 women finished PBP within 84 hours.

PBP is that for the former event the riders pay for everything in advance; the entry fee is large enough to cover refreshments at every control on an all-you-can-eat basis. For PBP, the entry fee does not include food or drink which has to be paid for separately. And having to pay for these things as you go adds a complexity that inevitably results in delays.

Having solved these logistical problems, we talked about things that happened over the last 2 to 3 days, and Heather gently probed for interesting anecdotes. At this point Alastair mentioned my stinging nettle incident, and I was forced to recount it. If you have seen the DVD you will already have enjoyed this highlight. If you haven't, then it is available from Damon at www.damonpeacock.com

We were a long time at the control in Carhaix, and it was growing dark before Alastair and I set out again. Stage 9 took us back to Loudeac, mostly following the same route as on the way out, but with three minor diversions, presumably for the sake of variety. One of these diversions was to the town of Rostrenen, whose name comes from the Bretton word *roz*, which means mound, and *draenen* which means brambles, so that the town is named after a hill of brambles. There's more to it than that, fortunately; the legend is that a wooden statue of the virgin, possibly with magical powers, was found in a bramble bush. The statue is exhibited in the church, but our route only skirted the outskirts of the town and we didn't take the time out to see it, nor to see the plaques erected in commemoration of ten resistance fighters hanged by the Nazis during the Second World War.

The final diversion ended when we rejoined the D53 at Saint-Martin-des-Prés, and I instantly recognised the impromptu café opposite the church. Alastair did not need any persuasion to stop, and we were soon sitting down to more sausage and drinking local cider. The *patron* here, a jolly and slightly inebriated woman, was enthusing about PBP and Brittany and her Breton identity, and listening to her was entertaining enough I had to have more cider and stay longer.

It was nice rolling country after that, and we had the wind at our backs, which made it pleasant riding. We arrived in Loudiac at 2 o'clock in the morning on 19th August.

At Loudiac I lost my glasses. Alastair and I shuffled through a small queue in the darkness to go through the control. Neither of us wanted to spend long here, and intended to refill bottles, perhaps grab a snack, and be off again. Because I can't see well enough close-up to read whilst wearing them, I took my glasses off. With my bottle in one hand and my helmet and my gloves and my glasses in the other, and my brevet card somewhere, and with the general state of my brain at this point... well you can imagine that something might go wrong.

Nothing seemed to go wrong, and the card was signed and I had something to drink and a flapjack, and with a minimum of fuss Alastair and I were cycling out of the control. As luck would have it, Bryan and Frank, who had obviously been there when we arrived, were leaving at the same time. I was delighted to be able to introduce Alastair to them.

We set off, confidently riding out into the night. But as soon as we swung out into country lanes, and I started to look beyond the close-up and well-lit surroundings of the control to the blurry hills under the indistinct stars of the night sky, I realised that I had forgotten my glasses.

I told my companions I would catch them up.

Back inside the control, I retraced my steps, fully expecting to find the glasses close to where we signed in. Or, failing that, close to where we'd picked up food. No sign. I tried to wake up my rusty French to explain the situation to the timekeepers. Fortunately the vocabulary, in particular, *lunettes* came back to me, and I managed to get a volunteer to make a note, describing the glasses — black plastic frames, prescription lenses that went dark in sunshine like sunglasses–and including my name, phone number, and email address.

And then I rushed back onto the road, hoping that at least I would catch my friends up. Twenty minutes later it was beginning to seem unlikely. I haven't timed it but I couldn't have spent less than ten minutes in the futile search for the glasses, and however slowly the others were cycling, I wasn't going to catch them unless or until they stopped somewhere.

After half an hour of cycling much faster than I was comfortable to, I managed to convince myself of this truth and settle down to a sustainable rhythm. A little later I went to take a sip of water, and noticed I had a bottle missing. Immediately I realised that my glasses would be with the missing water bottle where I had filled it up in Loudiac. There was nothing I could do about it now except to report this information at the next control.

I rode for another hour, and then when I reached the point I felt too tired to go on, I stopped by the side of the road, a convenient grassy area I deemed safe enough from cars. I drank half my remaining bottle of water with a cola flavoured caffeine tablet in it, and while I was drinking, got my bivvy bag ready. I crawled into the bag and went to sleep.

It was just about dawn when I woke up. I was stiff from lying on the hard ground, but otherwise quite refreshed. I rolled up the bivvy bag, stashed it in my pannier and got back on the road.

I met one of the X-men on the road into Tinténiac. He was a young American, and he was going slowly enough that when he reached me I could stay with him. He was dressed more like a racing cyclist than a randonneur. No wool. And he had caught me in 50 hours, having given me 11½ hours head start. This was a little humbling, but I drew some comfort from the fact that I was able to keep up with him without difficulty.

"You don't ride like a 90-hour rider," he told me. I think he meant it as a compliment.

What he failed to appreciate was that I could faff around like a champion couch potato in between bouts of cycling.

I was riding with this guy for ten minutes, and getting to know him, when he told me he had a hotel just here, and he stopped. I hadn't learnt his name and didn't remember his frame number, so I have no idea who he was. (Male cyclist, American, late 20s or early 30s, wearing a white jersey, for anyone who fancies some detective work. There were only 32 male American riders with X-numbers)

I rode the rest of the way into Tinténiac on my own, arriving at 9 o'clock in the morning. 867km done.

I reported my glasses once I had signed in at the control. I spent a while trying to communicate with a very sympathetic woman in her 40s, struggling to express myself clearly to convey the fact that the *lunettes*, which looked like sunglasses, had been left with a water bottle, a *bidon d'eau*. I was not helped by the fact that several Spanish words came obligingly to hand: *gafas, sol, agua.*

"*Parlez-vous anglais?*" she asked me.

When I said that I did, she started speaking English with a Glaswegian accent. Although she'd lived in this part of France for 30 years, she was Scottish. That established, it was relatively easy to communicate the sorry story of my glasses, and she obligingly phoned the control at Loudiac for me. We were waiting for a while as people at the other end of the phone were searching around, presumably in a box of lost property, but then she asked me to confirm the make of the water bottle, and of the glasses, and was able to tell me they had been found. It was possible that somebody would be able to transport them to Fougères for me to pick them up there.

Feeling very happy with myself, I sat down to a large breakfast.

Stage 11 to Fougères followed pretty well exactly the same route as Stage 4 in reverse. It was only 54km. I got there at 12:51, just under four hours after I arrived in Loudiac, so even allowing for a long breakfast, I didn't exactly rush. Moving east again, the landscape gradually grew less harsh; still rolling, but less so.

The streets were still lined with spectators, ordinary French people who saw cyclists on an epic journey as heroes. It is impossible to feel sorry for yourself when you're being cheered on by so many people. Everywhere along the route there was a carnival atmosphere.

At Fougères, my first priority was to ask after my glasses. Without them, the world was very slightly blurry. It wasn't a safety issue particularly, but it made the landscapes and scenery around me slightly less exciting. As the sun came up, I was squinting without the darkened lenses. If there was a need to read street signs I would have to slow down and really look at them.

So I asked, and waited, and asked, and was finally able to ascertain that they had not arrived here yet, that they wouldn't be coming here, but I would be able to collect them in Paris. Something of a shame, but that was the way it was. I could stop worrying about them until I arrived there myself.

I met Frank and Bryan as I was leaving Fougères, and we cycled the same 89km of roads as we had ridden on Stage 3. I asked about Alastair. Frank told me he'd been with them for a short while, but then had excused himself and dropped back, and they hadn't seen him again.

We stopped for a lengthy coffee in the same café in Lassay-les-Chateaux where we'd stopped before. I didn't realise it was the same town, much less the same café and indeed the same bloody table, until I had been sitting there for fifteen minutes. We had approached the place from the opposite direction, and I was sitting facing west this time, and that made it seem totally different.

Bryan somehow came adrift some time before Frank and I arrived at Villainess-la-Juhel at 7:25 in the evening with just over 1000km completed. 200km left to ride.

There was something of a festival going on in the town. Much more so than on the way out. Apparently at least 2000 people came out for it, partly to cheer on the cyclists, and partly because, well, once you've got a party, you've got a party. Lots of guests, lots of well-dressed people as well as cyclists and people cheering the cyclists. Nevertheless, I was keen to press on, but Frank was more laid-back, and wanted to see what was happening. So we wandered about for a while, finding food samples to eat, and a shot of very fine calvados to fortify the spirit.

Stage 13 was 81km to Mortagne au Perche, slightly shorter than Stage 3 on the way out. It was getting dark as we left, and my enthusiasm faded with the daylight. Early on I found I didn't have so much in my legs as I thought I had, and I was struggling to keep up with Frank, so much so that in the end I just let him go.

I cycled steadily through the night, slowly, but not that slowly. I stopped in a café somewhere and drank strong coffee. It was getting cold, so, having sat down somewhere warm, it was more difficult to get going again. But I did.

I arrived in Mortagne just after 1 o'clock in the morning. I was just over an hour inside my allocation at the time, but I was reading my brevet card which told me I was ten minutes over it. The times on the card were for a 17:15 start instead of 18:30, but I'd forgotten that. I wanted to press on, but after eating sufficiently I did one of Patrick's coffee stops, kipping for about 20 minutes on the floor before setting off again.

CHAPTER FOURTEEN

Bust

I cycled for an hour and a half before I started to feel tired again, and then it started raining. A thin rain, more dampening than anything else, but it was cold and miserable. For a while, however, it did keep me awake, and I cycled for another hour, and then I needed more sleep. I had one water bottle that was half empty and I put a couple of cola flavoured caffeine tablets into it, waited for it to stop fizzing, and drank it down. By this time I was inside bivvy bag, and out of the rain. I was asleep almost the moment I closed my eyes.

I woke up in the state of some agitated confusion. I was dreaming. In my dream MGL was sitting on top of me, urging me on, shouting at me, yelling at me for being useless, and I was unable to satisfy her. I woke up with mixture of shame, desperation, and confusion. As I woke up, the nightmare faded away, but I didn't know where I was, only that I was trapped. I needed to get out and I was sealed inside a plastic bag. My hands were pushing on the inside of the bag, searching for a way out.

My fingers found the zip, made an opening sufficient to let some air in and I could breathe. Gradually it dawned on me why I was lying in a bag in a field in the rain. I breathed deeply, concentrating on my breaths, until the panic in me died away.

When I was calm enough, I reflected on my cavalier attitude to body chemistry. I decided that caffeine was very much a drug to be careful with.

Still somewhat shaken, I got up, rolled up the bivvy bag, and stowed it, and got back on the bike.

A few minutes later a small group of cyclists caught me up and I cycled with them for a while. One of them was Dawn, or at least I thought it was. I thought so because she was an

American woman and she had music playing from her handlebars. I don't know if she remembered me from meeting me and Patrick what seemed a lifetime ago, and indeed I'm not sure if I remembered her or if this was somebody else, but I was glad of somebody to talk to.

I rode with these new cycling companions for perhaps half an hour before at some point I lost focus and they drifted up the road ahead of me, and by the time I realised this had happened, I didn't feel able to make up the distance.

It was still drizzling. Not enough to soak you, but enough to keep you damp. Increasingly, it was not raining enough to keep me awake. I met other cyclists of all nationalities. Sometimes I caught them up and passed them, other times they caught me up and then left me behind. Usually one of these two things or the other, but sometimes I would see the same faces and bicycles again and again.

I found myself closing my eyes from time to time, waking up with the start when the bike started to wobble. I was wondering how far it was to the next control, unable to see my bike computer in the dark. I would definitely have to sleep there.

Many non-cyclists think you have to balance a bicycle. It's not true, the bicycle balances itself. When you learn to ride a bike, you learn not to jerk it sideways enough to knock it over, you learn to allow it to stay balanced.

Many scientists who cycle believe it's the gyroscopic action of the wheels which keeps the bicycle upright. Something called the conservation of angular momentum means a spinning wheel will resist forces trying to change its axis of rotation. This is how a gyroscope or a spinning top stays upright.

Some cycling scientists recognise that something called trail is also responsible for bicycle stability. Trail is how, when you push a supermarket trolley, the wheels are kind of dragged behind and stay pointing in the right direction. The front wheel of the bike does that. It's because if you draw a line through the front forks and follow that line down to the ground you end up 20 cm or more front of the axle. The wheel *trails* behind the axis.

If you find an empty car park and take a bike and give it a huge push, you can watch it roll a hundred yards without falling over. As long as it's moving, it will remain stable. However, a bicycle whose handlebars are prevented from turning is unstable, and falls over, whether it's moving or not.

In 2009, a group at Cornell University developed a bike without any gyroscopic effect (each small wheel, front and back, was twinned with an identical wheel above it spinning in the opposite direction at the same speed) and without trail (the contact points of the front wheel actually slightly ahead of the steering axis). That this weird looking bike balanced just fine was due to another trick.

According to this team, what makes a bike balance is an ability to turn into a fall. If you've ever tried to balance a broom upside down on one finger[60], you will appreciate that as the broom falls, you have to move the supporting finger back underneath the centre of gravity. This is what a bike does. As it leans over, falling, the gyroscope effect turns the wheel, moving the support back underneath the bike. The trail helps make the bike follow the wheel. But the Cornell team managed to accomplish this just by making the centre of gravity of the rear of the bike higher than that of the front wheel and steering assembly, so that on leaning, the front falls faster, hence turning the wheel. If this effect is robust enough, trail is not necessary.[61]

What I think is cool about the story is that the basic bike hasn't changed since the invention of the safety bike over 100 years ago, and we are still learning some of the details about how it works.

The point of this digression is that you can fall asleep while riding a bicycle and you will still remain upright. That is, unless you slow to a stop, which you are likely to do unless you can dream about cycling, or the road turns and you fail to turn with it, which is inevitable if you don't slow to a stop.

I was riding with a group of French riders I had caught up with. When feeling confident, and wide awake, I have been known to speak inaccurate French semi-fluently, but now the most I could manage was "*bonsoir*". Except there was one rider sporting a rather accurate scale model of the Eiffel Tower on his cycle helmet, so to him I said, "*chapeau*," in admiration, but also kind of pathetically pleased with myself for the pun. I imagine however he'd heard this before.

I pulled away from these riders, during one of those moments where I tried to see if an increased physical effort could help me stay awake. It could not. A couple of minutes later I closed my eyes once again, and didn't open them until road went around a bend and I didn't, and the shock of bumping off the carriageway jolted me awake. Awake, but not in sufficient time to regain control of the bike before I rolled down a shallow ditch and up the bank on the other side to collide gently with a stone wall.

"*Chapeau!*" Eiffel Tower called cheerily as he went past.

---

[60] And if you haven't, you should.

[61] Check out their video: http://www.cornell.edu/video/andy-ruina-explains-how-bicycles-balance-themselves

I was standing astride my bike, my front wheel up against the low wall that surrounded a farm field, my rear wheel in the ditch I had ridden across. To my right, the French cyclists were riding away into the distance, their rear lights twinkling in the rain.

I was in a state of despair.

I knew without a doubt I wasn't going to make it. I could not continue without sleeping, and I needed proper sleep, not another 15 minutes here and there, and I didn't have time to do that and arrive back in Paris within my time limit. I was already behind schedule.

I got off my bike painfully, and brought it back to the road. I pedalled on, but now I was looking for a safe place to lie down, and I was crying, tears rolling down my face, only to be washed away by the rain.

Judicious study of the map and of Google Earth, particularly Street view, shows me that the wall was in the village of Maillebois, and is the perimeter wall of the fifteenth century Chateau de Maillebois, and that I somehow managed a further ten kilometres before finding a place to lie down, although as far as my memory is concerned, it was only a couple of minutes between crashing into the wall and finding somewhere to crash safely.

I found what turned out to be the perfect spot beside the church in the village of Crécy-Couvé. My face still wet with tears, I threw the bicycle down on the grass, snatched the bivvy bag out of a pannier and crawled inside it, not even bothering to take my shoes off. I heard myself sniffling pathetically a couple of times and then I was gone.

My final sleep stop on PBP 2015

CHAPTER FIFTEEN

Completion

It was daylight when I woke up, and warmer, and when I unzipped the bag, I could see it had stopped raining. I felt much better. I shuffled myself into a sitting position and took stock.

"*Bonjour*!"

I turned to see a young man leaning out of the window of the house beside the church, the window with the blue shutters.

"Bonjour," I replied, warily. I was expecting the next thing the man said to be something negative about me sleeping like a tramp underneath his window.

"*Ca va?*" the man went on, very hospitably. "*Voulez-vous quelque chose?*"

I understand that much French. I could also understand by the man's body language that he was indeed being friendly rather than sarcastic. When I hesitated, he suggested coffee and I couldn't say no to that.

Shortly afterwards, I was inside the house, getting to know him, his wife, and their young son, all of whom were about to have breakfast. I joined them. The coffee was excellent, as were the chocolate pancakes and the orange juice. The hospitality was overwhelming, and couldn't have come at a better time. The boy, I got to understand, had spent half the previous day cheering cyclists from outside the house, and nobody objected to a particularly smelly one inside the house.

When I told them I didn't think I'd be able to reach the finish in time, they assured me that it was only 70km or so to the finish and we looked at my brevet card together. At this point I remembered I had an hour and 15 minutes more than the time printed there, and it certainly seemed very possible. When this young family cheered me away, I was utterly determined to finish.

It was only another 11km to Dreux and I arrived there like a man possessed, overtaking a very surprised Patrick on the approach to the control. I shouted hello to him, but such was my

131

mental state that I deemed it necessary to sprint towards the timekeeper without slowing down to chat. It was about 8:20 in the morning. I was actually a little within my allocation, and not only that, I was well fed and well rested. From here it was only 64km to the end and I knew I was going to make it.

Patrick decided he needed some rest and some refreshment. I didn't, and I had a renewed sense of purpose. I told him I would meet him at the finish.

I averaged 21.7 km/h over those final 65km, a shade under three hours in the saddle, and arrived at Saint Quentin at 11:50 on the 20th August, having completed PBP in 88 hours and 50 minutes. On the way I caught up with Frank and Bryan and a few other people, most of them American, so I finished in something of a little peleton.

As we got closer, it seemed there were more and more people lining the streets. And then, rather suddenly, we were there, approaching the entrance to the velodrome through a crowd that disappeared as soon as we went through the gate. Now the driveway was defined by metal barriers on either side, corralling us towards the desk where we would get our cards stamped for the last time.

I looked at my watch. We were going to be inside 89 hours. Respectable enough.

"You are going to be too early for your Adrian Hands," Frank said to Bryan.

"Maybe I'll hang around a bit," Bryan said. He needed another five minutes.

"Wouldn't that be cheating?" I asked.

But at that moment we were wheeling our bicycles forwards and there was the clank of the electronics registering our ankle sensors and it was too late. Frank and I laughed at Bryan's expense and we propped our bikes up against the scaffolding that held the canopies up and presented our brevet cards.

In fact we surrendered our cards. After final approval by ACP office staff they would be posted out a couple of weeks later. We gave up the ankle devices too. At this point we were free. Finished.

We took selfies.

The author, Frank and Bryan feeling elated.

There was a big bike park now where three days earlier there had been the bike check area. There were no bike stands still vacant, and no space against a wall to lean a bike up, so the three of us propped our bikes up one against the others and followed an instinct that drew us into the velodrome itself.

Because here was refreshment. Snacks and coffee and beer. On the way we met Bryan's wife, Jo, who hugged him fiercely, as if he had had a wash in the last 48 hours.

Awhile later I slipped away and retrieved my left luggage, and armed with that I went down into the bowels of the building to find the shower room. Clean, and in fresh clothes, I felt a lot better.

I found the lost property area and asked after my glasses. Now that I'd eaten something, and rested, my ability to communicate in French was improved remarkably. However the glasses had not turned up yet. The man I spoke to thought it very likely they might do later on that evening.

I could do anything I wanted, and I wanted to do was to sleep. I laid out my camping mat and sleeping bag on the concrete outside the velodrome, and crawled into the bivvy bag on top of them. I slept for a couple of hours, until the sun came out in the late afternoon and it was too hot to sleep.

But I was hungry again by now.

Back inside, as luck would have it, and I certainly didn't plan this, I was just in time for the end-of-event meal. I hadn't actually read all my email from the PBP organisers or I'd have known this. It was posh buffet do, with plates and cutlery and everything.

I saw Richard Evans, and, congratulated him on the round the world trip as well as PBP. He'd started in the first group and had finished the evening before, enjoyed a night in a hotel room, and was dressed as a civilian, albeit in the tan colours favoured by world travellers. I might have been wearing jeans and a shirt, but under it I had cycling shorts, and my only footwear had cleats.

I saw Alastair and went over to talk to him. He was with a couple of other Dulwich Paragon riders, but he looked rough.

"I didn't make it," he said, almost as if he didn't quite believe it himself. He'd had a wretched time since I last saw him at Loudiac, coming down with some kind of illness. He'd gone to see a doctor at Fougères, and they had kept him an hour and a half to see one, not allowing him to continue until he had. The doctor had given him some pills he would probably have been able to pick up himself at a chemist, and he'd continued, but the waiting, in addition the slower progress he made while suffering, meant that he'd finished out of time. We chatted for a while and then he excused himself, saying he was going to go to his hotel to sleep.

I joined Richard and his friends, most of them London cyclists, for the meal. These guys were all intending to cycle back to Dieppe to catch the same ferry I was booked on, and were happy for me to ride with them.

There were some speeches, mostly in French, but some in English. A lot of people spoke, most of them important dignitaries of one form or another, most of them saying thank you to somebody or other, and what a great occasion this was. I was more interested in the food and the drink, as were the people immediately around me, and with well-timed excursions to the buffet table, there was plenty of food and drink to be had. I was now feeling very good indeed.

I bumped into Frank again outside the velodrome. He was catching a train later that evening back to Holland. He asked me how I was going to get home. I told him I was staying the night here, and that I would ride home if I felt strong enough tomorrow. Otherwise I would take a train.

"I think you will take the train," he said.

"I'm feeling good at the moment."

"I still think you will take the train."[62]

I met Richard and a group of riders from south-west London later in the evening for another meal and some drinking. There was no difficulty for me, or for anybody else around the table, to eat a second meal within a couple of hours of the previous one. I believe I ate a large pizza and had a number of beers, and there was loud happy conversation all around.

After eating, I excused myself, and cycled back to the velodrome, having remembered my glasses. Most of the lights were off, and it all looked very empty, but there was a side door open and I went inside, and then down to the centre of the velodrome where the lost property desk was. There was nobody around, so I ducked under the table and started looking through some boxes.

At this point a volunteer came in and wanted to know what I was doing.

For some reason, during the evening my powers of French conversation had diminished once again, and I had difficulty explaining why it was perfectly reasonable for me to have walked in off the street and be poking my nose around. As a result of this difficulty, the poor man was starting to get angry. I managed to apologise, and to say that I was very tired, and I could see he was very tired, and somehow I was able to communicate that I was not an opportunist thief and was genuinely looking for an item of lost property. My own lost property, in fact. He told me to come back tomorrow morning, and I agreed that was probably a good idea. The velodrome would be open by about 7 o'clock.

I went back to the restaurant to rejoin my dinner companions.

At the end of the evening, there was a general agreement to meet at 8 o'clock the following morning to start riding back to Dieppe for the ferry. Somebody asked me where I was staying, and I said I would probably go back to the campsite. Fortunately for me, Richard had a room to himself in the Formule 1 hotel, the friend he was going to share it with having already

---

[62] A few days later, we had this conversation on Facebook messenger:
 Frank: Hi, did you take the train or the ferry?
 Me: You won't believe me anyway.
 Frank: It's what you believe... I believe in the big train in the sky.

set off northwards that afternoon. So I ended up getting a double bed to myself while Richard had the bunk above it.

The alcohol I had consumed made it difficult to feel the pain in my legs and I didn't stay awake very long trying to feel it.

I was at the velodrome at 7:30 the next morning. The doors were locked, but after I had walked around the outside of the building checking all the other doors, somebody opened one and invited me in. The place was still pretty empty, but there were a couple of people about clearing things away. I was led into a back room where a number of cardboard boxes were lined up on the floor. The boxes contained various items of cycling equipment, mostly rainjackets, water bottles, and gloves. There was at least one cycle helmet. A young woman with a round face came out and asked me what I was looking for. When I told her, she disappeared again, and after a couple of minutes I wondered if I'd scared her off completely, but then she returned with the empty water bottle and my glasses attached to one another with black electrical tape.

"Merci beaucoup," I said, delighted.

My delight paled just a little when I realised that one of the lenses was missing.

I called the woman back, and, lacking the vocabulary for *lens* in French, communicated by pointing at the hole in the frame. She disappeared again, coming back a little later with the lens. She apologised that the glasses were broken, as if it was any fault of hers, and I assured her they would be easily fixed.

The glasses were wearable, and the loose lens for the most part stayed in place.

It was gone ten past eight by the time I was back outside, but only Richard was there at the meeting point so far, and it was a good 15 minutes before everyone was there ready to move. Eventually there were a magnificent seven riders assembled, and we set off boldly for England.

After twenty minutes we stopped for breakfast, a quantity of croissants and coffee setting the tone for the day, which was to be very much a gastronomic club run. The route, chosen by Phil, took us fairly directly north via quiet lanes, while Richard's contribution was choice of eating establishments, for which I have to say he has a talent. There was no hurry since the ferry wasn't until 10:30p.m. and we had all day to do 200km, which makes a very favourable comparison with the pace we'd needed for PBP. By lunchtime we were halfway there. I can't remember where halfway actually was, but there was a very acceptable *menu du jour*, which we washed down with liberal quantities of local cider. It is probably for the best that Normandy cider is served in wine glasses rather than tankards.

In the afternoon, Phil's route took us onto the *Avenue Verte*. I got to talking with Richard about the difference in cycle facilities in continental Europe and the UK. Richard works as a cycle lane adviser, or something like that. The comparison between the English and French sections of the *Avenue Verte* is obviously shameful, the English version often too convoluted and slow to be of use as a viable transport route, whereas the French one, benefitting from the vacant railway line, was fast and direct. Richard pointed out where it could nevertheless be improved; it crossed numerous small roads where you had to stop and check the road was clear, Giving Way to motor traffic. Richard would have given the cyclist right of way here; the cyclist might be travelling long distance, possibly as we were doing, Paris to London, albeit at a cyclist's pace, whereas the motor traffic was mostly local, making short journeys. When the route had been a railway line, the cars had obviously stopped for the trains.

There were frequent breaks where we stopped for refreshment or to wait for slower members of the group to catch up. I was delighted I was not among this number — not all of my companions had been sub-80 hour PBP finishers. At one such stop I left my glasses behind. I noticed five minutes later and knew right away that I'd left them on top of a wooden fence next to a gate where we'd been sharing chocolate. Clearly I had needed to take them off to look at the map on my phone or something.

The others said they'd ride on slowly but I found out the name of the restaurant they were heading for in Dieppe just in case.

Of course, by the time I'd spent five minutes cycling in the opposite direction, found the glasses exactly where I'd left them and turned around, I was ten minutes behind, and this is a considerable gap. I suffer from totally unrealistic optimism syndrome, and therefore pushed myself to catch them, stubbornly believing it was possible. I was driving myself along the cycle path like I was time trialling, and it hurt.

Once the *Avenue Verte* left the conveniently flat and direct railway line, presumably because here the line was still in use by trains, I wasted some time in navigating. As the route retrieved from Pocket Earth on my phone took me up to the village of Martin-Église, high above the railway line and with a view of the Port of Dieppe, I realised I wasn't going to catch anyone, so I relaxed and concentrated on enjoying the ride. It was drawing dark as I made my way into the city, but I followed the instructions I'd been given and got to the waterfront at least without difficulty. Finding the restaurant itself was harder, and even with the help of Google Maps it wasn't straightforward, but happily, once I was close enough, I met a couple of English cyclists who were meeting my companions at the same restaurant and that solved the problem for me.

There were two or three hours before we needed to be on the ferry, and the restaurant of choice, a small friendly affair with great seafood, was the place to do it. We ate and drank and ate and drank some more, and then had strong coffee to enable sufficient concentration to get to the ferry.

On the ferry we met Steve Abraham. Steve was heading for the cabin a well-wisher had booked for him, his sleep in pursuit of the One Year record being something precious. The rest of the English cycling contingent, perhaps another half-dozen besides the guys I'd ridden with that day, distributed themselves around the available impromptu sleep-friendly floorspace. My own accommodation, with inflatable foam mat and sleeping bag, amounted to luxury.

When I awoke, the ferry was making the enormous noise that ferries do when they line themselves up for docking. There was enough time to pack up my sleeping kit and get a cup of tea and then it was time to disembark.

In Newhaven, different cyclists went different ways, leaving Richard and I to cycle the rest of the way to Raynes Park in South West London together, Richard showing me a better route, though perhaps one less exciting, than the one I'd used on the way out. At six o'clock on a summer morning, the roads were quiet, which made the cycling a dream, but equally it made breakfast elusive.

At 7a.m. we found a newsagent just opening in the village of Ardingly, and there was a hope it might provide refreshment, perhaps even coffee. It didn't, but, even better, it provided golden information about the bakery around the corner. Said bakery was just off the main road through the village, so you wouldn't notice it normally unless you knew.

It wasn't quite open yet, but as soon as the morning staff saw us, we were welcomed inside. It was a magical world for a hungry cyclist, the shelves lined with good things, the air full of the beautiful smell of bread and pastries. And they had a coffee machine. We spent half an hour there, eating pastries, drinking coffee, learning about the appropriately named proprietor Mr Bunn, and answering questions about what we'd done, while they set the shop up for the day around us.

After that it was easy cycling. The sun was out and we didn't need our outer layers of GoreTex. We both felt we could keep riding forever, although I thought such a good feeling was probably best not put to the test. Instead, we decided to end our ride with a stop at the Raynes Park Weatherspoon's for a pint of beer and a cooked breakfast. It was 9a.m.

Contrôle	Km	Temps	Passage	Moyenne tronçon	Moyenne Totale
START	0		16/08 16:51		
VILLAINES	221	11:37	17/08 06:30	19 km/h	19 km/h
FOUGERES	310	16:17	17/08 13:48	13.3 km/h	16.9 km/h
TINTENIAC	364	21:43	17/08 16:15	15.8 km/h	16.7 km/h
LOUDEAC	449	27:15	17/08 21:41	15.5 km/h	16.5 km/h
CARHAIX	525	36:17	18/08 06:44	8.3 km/h	14.4 km/h
BREST	618	41:33	18/08 12:24	16.4 km/h	14.7 km/h
CARHAIX	703	48:10	18/08 18:41	13.5 km/h	14.5 km/h
LOUDEAC	782	55:38	18/08 01:59	10.8 km/h	14 km/h
TINTENIAC	867	62:25	19/08 08:55	12.2 km/h	13.8 km/h
FOUGERES	921	66:20	19/08 12:51	13.7 km/h	13.8 km/h
VILLAINES	1009	72:52	19/08 19:23	13.4 km/h	13.8 km/h
MORTAGNE	1090	78:31	20/08 01:02	14.3 km/h	13.8 km/h
DREUX	1165	85:52	20/08 08:23	10.2 km/h	13.5 km/h
FINISH	1230	88:51	20/08 11:22	21.7 km/h	13.8 km/h

My official stage times and average speeds from the PBP website. On eight of the fourteen stages I averaged a lower speed than was necessary overall.

CHAPTER SIXTEEN

Catford CC Hill Climb

I had an idea for a final challenge for the cycling year, following what I perceived as my success in the Mersey Roads 24, and in completing PBP. This would be another historic, but otherwise very different, sporting event. The Catford CC Hill Climb.

This is, in fact, the oldest continuously running cycling event in the world, having started in 1887. (The second oldest is PBP.) It takes place nowhere near Catford, which used to be a small town to the south of London and is now a less salubrious area of South East London, but out in the Wolds of Kent on the very steep Yorks Hill. Which is nowhere near York, although to go up the climb you move in a northerly direction, which is roughly towards that city.

My previous encounter with the event was when I visited it as part of a charity ride organised by Charlie in aid of Breast Cancer research. She called the ride "Twin Peaks", and a friend of hers created a poster in which two cupcakes resembled a pair of breasts. The twin peaks that allowed for such innuendo were the climbs of Yorks Hill and White Lane, on which were based the hill climb events of Catford CC and Bec CC respectively. The two hill climbs are traditionally on the same day, one in the morning and the other in the afternoon, to allow competitors and spectators to do both. Charlie's ride began at her partner's café on Old Street in central London and went out to each event in turn. Some of Charlie's teammates competed, and one of them, Lydia Boylan, won both competitions. At the time, I was nowhere near fit enough to give the event a decent stab, and proved it to myself a month later when I returned there and all but failed to get up the climb without walking. Now, I thought, I would do better.

As the school holidays finished, and I reacquainted myself with the world of paid employment, I used my commute for a bit of training, travelling to and from my school via Downs Road in Wimbledon, which is the steepest hill for miles around, although it rather lacks the length of Yorks Hill. While my average monthly mileage dropped from its August peak, I told myself what really mattered was keeping the strength in the legs for the short burst.

I had repaired my Bianchi bike after the 24, having to replace the handlebar stem entirely because the bolts could neither be tightened nor removed. The replacement stem was not expensive, but it was a frustrating business when I ordered a stem of the wrong diameter and had to return it. While I was at it I replaced the handlebar tape and made some other cosmetic improvements to the bike. I was looking forward to racing it again.

Unfortunately, I came down with a cold two weeks before. I was off work with it for a couple of days, and then, whilst fit enough to go back, I didn't feel up to riding a bike more than the degree necessary to get me to and from work. By the weekend of the event, I was feeling a lot better, and I believed I was more or less up to the challenge.

So, on the second Sunday in October, I cycled out from home the 50km to the North Downs in Kent, following more or less the route of Charlie's charity ride, which I'd downloaded onto my phone. I arrived early enough I could enjoy the atmosphere. There was some atmosphere to enjoy, with a sizable crowd of people milling about in the car park at the top of the hill, a refreshment stall, and the sound of a commentator broadcast through loudspeakers. There were spectators lining the final few hundred metres of the course. I took advantage of some fast food on offer, and ride-enhancing coffee, and then rode down and up the hill for a recce. As I got close to the top, the first rider was coming up the slope. He was a man of perhaps my own age, riding, or attempting to ride, a fixed-wheel bike. He was struggling desperately, and at one point came to a standstill and was held upright by a spectator.

"Am I allowed to push you?" the spectator asked.

"No, but do it anyway!"

After which, I no longer felt so well-prepared.

Ascertaining that there was no requirement to wear a helmet for the event, at least for those over 18, deemed responsible enough to make informed decisions about their own safety, I left mine with one of the event organisers, together with my water bottles, pump, tool kit, rainjacket, and even my keys in an effort to reduce the weight I had to lift up the hill. The commentator was telling everyone that the best riders all managed less than three minutes, and that this was a remarkable achievement. For some reason this man's voice made me feel that, by virtue of the amount of cycling I had done this year, I ought to be capable of the same.

There was no rational reason for me to think this.

Feeling a little nervous, I made my way carefully down the hill, stopping and pulling in to the side whenever a competitor came up the road. The crowd of spectators, thick at the top, thinned out as I went down, until there were only one or two bystanders in spots where the road was wider, and then there were none. I passed the timekeeper with his deckchair and stopwatch, and there were two riders ready to go one minute and two minutes in front of me warming up. I cycled on a little way and I was in a quiet country lane in late summer, the event out of sight and out of earshot.

I was almost tempted to continue riding, leaving the noise and the fear of competition behind me. Instead, I made slow circuits, riding up and down the same 50 metres of road, until it was my time, and I rode up to the timekeeper and presented myself.

For my second time-trial start in 30 years I needed to be more energetic than my first. I pushed on the pedals with everything I had, and surged forwards. I built up speed and was quickly spinning my legs, wanting to change up a gear. Anticipating the road steepening, I did not. All too soon, the gradient was there, and my legs slowed up, protesting. I changed down, and kept moving.

I could feel the pain in my legs, the blood pounding in my ears, my face hot with effort. I felt the thrill of competition. There was time to think I was doing well, before my breath started to fail. I couldn't get the air into me fast enough. I began to fade.

As I came up to the first spectators, shouts of encouragement gave me a boost that sent me around the next curve in the road, then I faded again, and I struggled until the road levelled out slightly half way up the hill. I needed to build speed up while I could but lacked the strength to do it. Nevertheless, when the road steepened, there was a crowd there to cheer and I gave it my best shot.

Towards the top, Yorks Hill becomes insanely steep, becoming 1 in 4 shortly before the riders get sight of the finish. By now, my stopwatch already beyond three minutes, I felt defeated, already disappointed with my time while my time was still getting worse, but the shouted encouragement forced me to keep digging. I gave 100%.

But my 100% wasn't as impressive as I'd wished. I reached the finish line barely moving, and rolled to a halt. This is the kind of hill climb where there are volunteer "catchers" who grab hold of riders who have so spent themselves with physical effort that they are unable to stay balanced on their bikes, and I took advantage of this service. My stopwatch said I'd taken 3 minutes 25 seconds, but it felt much longer than that.

I climbed off my bike, thanked my catcher, and then went and sat on a grass verge for a few minutes. For a long while I thought I was going to throw up, but I didn't. My chest hurt and I was coughing painfully, and this went on for a few minutes. Eventually I got to my feet and wandered across to where I'd left my things so I could put a rainjacket on before I felt cold. I bought myself a cup of tea and heaped sugar into it.

This helped. I began to feel better, but then I was standing in front of the scoreboard watching as new times were marked up on it as they were relayed over, almost all of them faster than mine. I decided to cut my losses and head for home. I could find out that I'd come 114th out of 122 finishers at a later date.

It was a lovely autumn day, warm in the sunshine, and with little wind. It was perfect for cycling. I felt totally drained, but I could happily turn the pedals over, even it was beyond me to put any significant pressure on them. I made my way homewards at a gentle pace.

I was glad of the directions on my phone mounted to the handlebars because the last thing I felt I had the energy for was to navigate the best way home. And I was almost there when disaster struck.

In hindsight, it was a poor idea to use a short cut along part of the River Wandle footpath while riding a lightweight road bike with narrow tyres. Particularly when I was so tired. But that is what I was doing. And I was unlucky that in my less-than-100% state I was presented with a distraction and at the same time a hazard to my progress.

The distraction was a man sitting on the footpath, in a place where you would not expect a person to be sitting. We should be wary of making snap judgements, but even from a distance and while I was riding a bicycle, he looked like a homeless person. The hazard was a web of tree roots that rippled under the thin tarmac of the path.

I didn't notice the tree roots until my front wheel twisted under me, and I was falling. My eyes registered a blur of movement as the green of the trees all around and the blue of the sky wheeled around me, and the next thing I knew I was on the ground.

I sat up uncertainly. My bike was a short distance away. It looked undamaged, and my phone was miraculously still attached to the handlebars. Bizarrely, the phone being new, it was the first thing I was concerned about. I didn't think I had broken anything, but I couldn't feel any pain yet, only shock. My elbow was bleeding profusely.

Ten feet away from me, the homeless man was getting unsteadily to his feet.. There was a can of cider on the path beside him.

"Man, you had a *crash*," he said, somewhat unnecessarily. His voice was slurred, and he was clearly drunk.

He came towards me, his hands out to help me up. I got to my feet quickly to prevent this happening. I was suddenly aware of my open wounds, and had to turn to prevent him touching them. He clearly meant well, but I didn't think he was in a position to help me.

"Man, you are *fucked up!*" he told me. "I thought I was fucked up, but you're worse than me."

"I'm okay," I said, starting to feel nauseous. I picked up my bike. It looked okay. The new handlebar tape was scuffed and the brake levers were both at the wrong angle, but the wheels looked true and there was nothing else obviously wrong.

"You don't look good. Man, you took a fall."

"I'm okay," I said. I climbed back on the bike, my hip hurting as I did, causing me to notice a big hole in my cycle shorts and grazed flesh inside it. I rode very slowly along the path, each turn of the pedal hurting my hip, and I continued for two hundred yards to the end of the path where it came out into a side road. Here I was out of sight of the man, and I stopped and sat on the kerb for a few minutes, taking stock, and waiting for the shock to subside a little.

I was basically okay, I thought. My elbow was bleeding quite a lot, but not so much I would run out of blood, and everything else was superficial. And I was only two or three miles from home.

MGL moaned at me for dripping blood on the floor, but then insisted on helping me wash the wound. In the bathroom, the sink was stained bright red with the blood, and she told me there was a quantity of gravel to be cleaned out. Then she put a bandage on it and told me she thought we needed to go to Accident and Emergency.

Accident and Emergency is not my favourite place to go. It's full of people feeling sorry for themselves or who are made irritable by pain, it is a place of confusion and uncertainty, and

144

the aesthetics are terrible. And, unless you go in complaining of chest pains, or you have a small child with you, you will be in for a long wait. Nevertheless, when blood started leaking out of the bandage, and MGL changed it, and then blood started leaking out again half an hour later, it was clear that we had to go.

So we spent part of the evening in St George's Hospital in Tooting, and enjoyed hot chocolate from the dispenser, and my arm was seen to by a nurse and then a doctor and then by a couple of plastic surgeons who happened to be around. I was unable to see what the plastic surgeons did, because while they worked on my elbow the angle was wrong for me to look, but MGL said she was very impressed with the needlework. It took them a good twenty minutes of stitching; apparently, the hole in my elbow was half a centimetre deep and there wasn't much flesh there to sew into.

I spent much of the next week wearing a sling, and had to go to work by train.

EPILOGUE

In 2015 I cycled 9200km, or 5800 miles, more than I had ever done before, and this despite hardly touching the bike except for commuting to work after the Catford CC Hill climb.

Steve Abraham cycled 63,608 miles, short of Tommy Goodwin's record, but impressive in the circumstances, or in any circumstances. He decided, mid-year, to keep going, aiming to beat Goodwin's yearly total on a rolling year from August 2015 to July 2016, but eventually gave up on this.

Kurt **Searvogel** did break the record, achieving a very impressive 76,076 miles 76 years after Tommy Goodwin. The record only lasted a year, because at the time of writing Amanda Coker has just smashed the record with 86,537 miles.

Tom Davies completed his round the world trip, taking 174 days, raising £60 000 for charity, and finding himself in newspapers and in front of TV cameras for a week. Nobody has contradicted his claim to be the youngest person to ride around the world.

Richard Evans wrote a book about his round-the-world trip, called *Laid Back Around the World*, or, less concisely, Laid Back Around the World in 180 Days: Diary of a long bike ride, which I can recommend, especially since all Richard's profits are going to the charity Road Peace, the national charity for road crash victims.

Sadly, my friend Charlie passed away in September 2016. I feel privileged to have known her, and have remembered her very fondly where she has occurred in this memoir.[63]

---

[63] This obituary in the Telegraph gives you an idea what she was like, http://www.telegraph.co.uk/obituaries/2016/09/08/charlotte-easton-inspirational-classics-teacher--obituary/, and this one, on the Rapha website, containing her own words, and those of her husband Sam, http://pages.rapha.cc/feature/charlotte-easton is amazing.

GLOSSARY

AAA This is a type of small battery delivering 1.5V for various portable electronics. In the world of audax, the three As stand for Audax Altitude Award, but it can't be an accident that the letters look a bit like a mountain range. For every thousand metres of climbing in an audax event, there is one AAA point. Riders who succeed in achieving 20 or more points in a single season can get a badge.

Audax. Essentially an activity that involves cycling set distances, usually upwards of 100km and always measured in kilometres, at a speed between a maximum speed, generally 30km/h, and a minimum, generally 15km/h but sometimes 13⅔ or even 12km/h for longer events. The sport originated in Italy and France and is organised in the U.K. by Audax UK.

Brevet Card This is a piece of card a cyclist carries with her when taking part in an audax. At each control she presents it to be stamped, often with a heartwarming cartoon image or a message of encouragement. Between controls it is stuffed in a pocket or into a plastic wallet hanging around the neck under the cycling jersey. In hot or wet weather (i.e. pretty much all the time) it will end up soggy and somewhat worse for wear.

Cadence The drop in pitch of the voice, especially at the end of a sentence. Also how fast a cyclist is pedalling, usually measured in revolutions per minute.

Chapeau. This is French for hat. Although hats are not as ubiquitous nowadays as they once were, the word *hat* remains a useful one in many languages. Just as the salute is a gesture of respect derived from the action of removing the hat as a courtesy, the French use the word *chapeau* in similar fashion. Where a young English person might say "respect!" a French person might say "*chapeau!*" Since French is the lingua franca of the international pro cycling world, the expression has been borrowed into English.

Clipless Pedals Once upon a time cyclists who wanted a little more in terms of pedalling efficiency used metal clips which went around the front of the foot and had a leather strap to hold the foot tight against the pedal, so the rider could not only push down on them but push forwards and pull upwards. With a cleat on the bottom of a specialised cycling shoe as well, the rider could pull or push the pedal through every part of its cycle.

Then somebody who both cycled and skied realised that the same effect could be achieved more conveniently and more economically (in terms of weight if not money) by using the kind of attachments common between skis and ski boots instead of cycle clips. These new attachments, which you might call clips if you didn't know any better, are part of a system called clipless pedals as they do away with the need for (the previous generation of) cycle clips.

Control This is a place where a willing volunteer records the names of each rider who arrives, together with their time of arrival, and who also stamps or initials the all-important brevet card. The control may be in a café or a village hall that is providing refreshments, or it may be a roadside lay-by. Sometimes it is a shop where the shopkeeper agrees to do the brevet card stuff knowing that hungry cyclists will buy enough junk food to keep the business afloat for another day. Sometimes there is a control with nobody there and it's called an information control.

Cycle Computer When I was about 12 my brother and I discovered some fairly cheap milometers in a bike shop. They mounted at the front hub, and they had a small plastic cog wheel that engaged with the front spokes where they emerged from the hub. They made a loud clicking sound in operation and, since they had no provision for adjustment for different bicycles, were only very approximate, but they did enable us to measure and therefore boast of the mileages we did on summer afternoons. When more sophisticated apparatus became available in the 1990s, utilising integrated electronic circuits, and measuring wheel revolutions by the induced voltage spikes as a small magnet spun past a sensor on the bicycle fork, so dispensing with annoying clicks and associated friction, their manufacturers called them cycle computers, and the cycling public let them get away with it. The totality of the available computation might be speed, trip distance, total distance, average speed and maximum speed, and yet we use the same word we use for a device that can beat a world champion at chess, reckon the best travel route between any two addresses or keep a teenager entertained for 48 hours at a stretch. Still, they're quite handy.

Cyclecross This is a sport for people who like mud. More specifically those who like bicycles, mud and suffering. The idea is very simple, a bicycle race around an off-road circuit. In reality the off-road circuit generally starts off muddy, and after a couple of laps is treacherously so. There are gradients too steep to cycle up, so competitors have two run with their bikes, and there are sometimes obstacles like logs in the way so that a degree of bicycle acrobatics is necessary. Oh, and people do it in winter so it's nice and cold. A dedicated cyclocross bike looks like an ordinary racing bike except it will have cantilever or disc brakes and wide clearance in the frame to avoid the likelihood of the wheels being jammed with mud. Mountain bikes are permitted, but generally they are not quite as fast as a cyclocross bike. The sport was invented before the mountain bike, and while there are similar mountain bike competitions, there is a slightly different philosophy.

Dropout – somebody who really isn't cut out for the rigours of either academic study or the rat race of life in general. Also, it's that part of the bike where the wheel fits in. If you loosen the wheel attachments and hold the bike up, if you're lucky, the wheel "drops out". On old-fashioned bikes, the one at the back was horizontal so that you could change the distance between the back wheel and where the pedals are. This lets you keep the chain fastened tight, even if you don't have some kind of spring mechanism to tighten it. This sort of thing is very important to some people.

Fettle – According to my dictionary, to fettle is to line or repair the walls of a furnace, or something similar to a furnace. It is also slang for making minor adjustments to a machine, a bicycle, for example, to optimise its performance.

Fixed – held together, mended. Or in this case the rotation of the back wheel is locked (fixed) in sync with the rotation of the pedals. The alternative is a bike fitted with a freewheel.

A fixed gear bike is sometimes called a fixie by people who believe them to have magical properties. Almost necessarily, such a bike will also have no gears, or to be pedantic, have exactly one gear. On such a bike, it is necessary to pedal downhill as well as uphill, and if the rider stops pedalling, the bike will attempt to catapult them into the air. Really.

Such bikes are obligatory for track competitions. Explanations as to why people choose to ride them on the road include:

- Less is more. Without gears, there is less to go wrong, so you have more time to enjoy riding your bike, or read the newspaper, or whatever you normally do with the time you are not engaged in bicycle maintenance.
- They look cool. They look especially cool without mudguards. The fact that they are difficult and perhaps dangerous to ride, and that in wet weather you get a wet stripe up your bum is a small price to pay.
- It's like a Zen thing. I can't explain.

Freewheel To move without effort. The word comes from the cycle component, which is a ratchet mechanism connected to the gear sprocket or sprockets on the rear wheel such that when the rider pedals, the chain drives the rear wheel, but the wheel is free to go on rotating when the rider stops pedalling. Most bicycles have them, enabling the rider to push on the pedals when necessary, which is sadly most of the time, and relax when it is not. The alternative is a fixed wheel.

Information Control Information is a valuable commodity, and has always been controlled. Certain knowledge is jealously guarded by those who have it. But in the context of an audax event, the possession of a piece of information only available at a particular geographical location, for example, the date on a particular statue, is used to control the riders, in particular making sure they do indeed visit that location. You have to go to the statue to read the date, therefore you cannot take a shortcut missing this part of the course. Unless, of course, you ask somebody what the date was.

Randonneuring In French, audax and randonneuring denote two distinct versions of long-distance unsupported endurance cycling, a division that dates back to an acrimonious splintering of the movement a century ago. Outside France, the two words mean about the same thing. In the UK, everybody uses the word audax, in the USA they prefer randonneuring, although the word sounds a little poncey. The American organisation supporting endurance cycling is Randonneurs USA, or RUSA, which used to confuse me because it looks like it's something to do with Russia.

Recumbent Lying down, or, at the very least, reclining. A recumbent bike or trike has the rider sitting as if in a deck chair with the pedals in front of him or her. There are two advantages to this. Firstly, it puts the rider in a position where they can use their leg and back muscles more efficiently, and secondly, it is more aerodynamic. Recumbent bikes or trikes with a fairing to further reduce aerodynamic drag can be very fast indeed. Of course, there are disadvantages, which include cost, and the fact that any recumbent will be heavier than an ordinary bike built from the same materials. Recumbent bicycles tend to be less stable, at low speeds at least, and they do look just a tiny bit daft.

National Cycle Network The national cycling route network of the United Kingdom was established to encourage cycling throughout the country, as well as for the purposes of bicycle touring. It was created by the charity Sustrans who were aided by a £42.5 million National Lottery grant. The 14,000-mile network was used for over 230 million trips in 2005.

The NCN uses bridleways, disused railways, minor roads, canal towpaths and traffic-calmed roads in towns and cities. Dedicated bike paths are ideal, but at the moment the majority of the network is still on roads.

The network started with Bristol and Bath Railway Path (now part of National Route 4) in 1984, a 25km route along a disused railway. By August 2014, there were 23,700 km of cycle route signposted so that a reasonably savvy cyclist can follow them without a map or a GPS unit.

Pack – this is a bundle or a load, often carried on the back. As a verb it means to arrange clothing and/or other belongings into a bag or suitcase etc. To pack something in is to give up on it, presumably with the inference that the items of clothing and other belongings need to be arranged back into the luggage. In a cycling event, to pack means to give up, abandon the event, even if this action does not involve rearrangement of luggage.

Peloton Originally this was French for a small ball. It's clearly related to the English word pellet. The French word evolved to mean a group of things, especially people, and is the origin of the word platoon. It is also the word used in French and other languages specifically for a group of cyclists riding in a group so as to benefit from one another's slipstream and is a major feature of cycle races.

Permanent Something that is permanent is going to be around for a long time, if not longer. A permanent audax ride is one you can do, by arrangement with the organiser, any day or night of the year, provided you supply said organiser with proof you did indeed ride the course in the form of receipts or GPS data. I've never done one, so I'm the wrong person to ask for details.

Safety Bicycle A bicycle is intrinsically a pretty safe form of transport, certainly the safest vehicle other than no vehicle at all. Most of the danger to a cyclist comes from other vehicles, typically cars, and especially lorries.[64] It wasn't always so. Before the 1880s, most bicycles were high roller, or "Ordinary" bicycles, with a giant front wheel connected to the pedals, and a tiny trailing rear wheel.[65] The front wheel was enormous because without any gears, it needed a large circumference for the rider to achieve a decent speed at achievable cadence. Because the centre of gravity was so high, a collision with a bump in the road was likely to send the rider over the handlebars for a "header" and likely injury. Of course, to compensate for dangerous bicycles there was nothing in the way of dangerous motorised traffic. Around 1880 a number of inventors used a chain to connect a large chainwheel at the pedals with a smaller sprocket attached to the drive wheel, creating the bicycle without dangerously overlarge wheels, which was indeed, safe. Ten years later, the turn-of-the-century bicycle boom was in full swing.

Strava Social media hits the world of cycling (and running, I might mention.) Strava lets an athlete log where they ride or run by GPS, see their track on a map, either afterwards or on the screen of their GPS unit or phone, and then post it for their friends or for all the world to see. The world can even watch your progress live, if both you and the world consent. On Strava you can see how far and how fast your friends are going, and you can see how fast you have covered a particular stretch of road or path compared to other people. There are some riders who compete to achieve the status of KOM, King of the Mountain,[66] for a stretch of road, covering that small part of the world faster than anybody else. Or at least anybody else with Strava.

---

[64] Trucks, to readers of US English. Lorries turning left, or Trucks turning right, in either case are particularly dangerous to cyclists on their inside, when often the driver is totally unable to see where the vulnerable road user actually is. It is perfectly legal to drive heavy goods vehicles with such poor visibility.

[65] The nickname penny farthing, based on coins of the same relative sizes, came about long after the Ordinary bicycle was superseded.

[66] Of course, if you are a woman, you can compete for QOM. All this being on the internet, in cyberspace, you can compete to be Queen even if you are not a woman. For the purposes of Strava, a "mountain" may be flat, or even downhill.

Not surprisingly, in an intensive world, people can become obsessed with Strava. The expression "if it's not on Strava, it didn't happen", a comment related to the question of whether trees fall in forests when nobody sees them, is available on T shirts. There have been people killed trying to achieve KOM status on downhill sections of road. This is the world we live in.

Time Trial The race of truth, as the French call it. A time trial is a race against the clock. Generally, riders are set off at one minute intervals by a timekeeper and they ride the course, whatever course that might be, on their own. Unless we are talking about a team time trial, and we are not, it is absolutely forbidden to assist or to be assisted by anyone else, most obviously by drafting, where one rider rides behind the other, taking advantage of their slipstream. The rules state that you have to ride alone. If somebody overtakes you, you are not allowed to follow behind them, benefitting from their slipstream. In fact, you have to let them move ahead. If you find yourself catching them up shortly afterwards, and this hardly ever happens, you are obligated to wait a decent interval, some distance behind, before you overtake them again.

In the UK, the peculiar custom is for time trials of exactly 10, 25, 50 or 100 miles over a circuit, with a rule that the start and finish be no more than half a mile apart to avoid the like-lihood of benefit of a prevailing wind. Because riders are naturally keen to improve on their personal bests, the most popular courses tend to be those that plough up and down a busy main road, turning around a big roundabout at the halfway point. The smooth tarmac and the airflow produced by speeding automobiles apparently more than compensates for the unpleasantness and danger associated with cycling on a road otherwise avoided by cyclists.